THE WOMAN'S DAY BOOK OF GREAT SANDWICHES

Also by Diane Harris

THE WOMAN'S DAY BOOK OF BAKING
THE NO CHOICE DIET

DIANE HARRIS

THE Woman's Day BOOK OF GREAT SANDWICHES

Holt, Rinehart and Winston □ New York

I would like to thank Dina von Zweck and Ward Mohrfeld for their invaluable help and encouragement.

Published by Holt, Rinehart and Winston,
383 Madison Avenue, New York, New York 10017.
Published simultaneously in Canada by Holt, Rinehart and Winston of Canada, Limited.

Library of Congress Cataloging in Publication Data
Harris, Diane.
The Woman's day book of great sandwiches.
Includes index.
1. Sandwiches. 2. Cookery, International. I. Woman's day. II. Title.
TX818.H36   1982   641.8′4   81-20021
ISBN 0-03-061539-9   AACR2
ISBN 0-03-058967-3 (pbk.)

First Edition

Designer: Joy Chu
Illustrator: Laura Hartman

Printed in the United States of America
10 9 8 7 6 5 4 3 2 1

ISBN 0-03-061539-9 HARDBOUND
ISBN 0-03-058967-3 PAPERBACK

TO MY MOTHER AND FATHER

CONTENTS

INTRODUCTION

WALK INTO ANY POPULAR SANDWICH SHOP IN NEW ORLEANS, delicatessen in New York, or natural foods restaurant in San Francisco, and you'll discover a whole array of great-tasting sandwiches you've probably never had before. Just one experience like this makes you realize the exciting possibilities in the art of sandwich making. It's a food-lover's moment of awakening.

This book has been designed to give you that very same experience—to open the door to a whole new world of eating pleasure. So we have gathered a varied collection of some of the most imaginative and soul-satisfying sandwiches we could find. We've included time-honored classics as well as bright new creations. And they range from garden-fresh vegetarian delights to a standout recipe for the "perfect" hamburger.

Because we believe that the basis of good sandwiches is good bread, we also feature a variety of unusually fine bread recipes—hearty whole grain loaves, crusty rolls, buttermilk breads, sweet tea breads, and several nut-studded quick breads. We even offer a simple recipe for Middle Eastern pita. But you don't have to make your own loaves to have delicious

ix

and healthful breads. The supermarkets abound in interesting choices.

Attention to detail is the secret of success in sandwich making, as it is in anything else. Not only do you have to start with good bread, you also have to make sure you have the best spreads and garnishes. If herb-scented mayonnaise would add just the right finishing touch to a sandwich, then blend up a batch. If watercress would supply the perfect peppery note to a somewhat bland filling, use cress. If grated onion would make the difference between so-so and sensational, get out your grater. The end results clearly reflect this kind of meticulous care.

Obviously the heart of any sandwich is a perfectly seasoned, freshly made filling. And throughout the book we offer hints and recipes to ensure moist flavorful meat and egg fillings, crisp salad combinations, and fresh-tasting cheeses and cheese spreads. There are tips on how to season meat loaf so that it's just as good cold as it is hot, how to hard-cook eggs so that yellow and white look and taste delicious, how to poach chicken for the best flavor and texture. And there are hundreds of suggestions for great combinations that go way beyond ham and cheese.

Some of the world's great sandwiches seem created for entertaining. What could be more easygoing and enjoyable than a party built around sandwiches? And well-planned sandwich menus are suitable for festive brunches, great lunches, and imaginative dinners. We have included everything from a summer brunch that features French-Toasted Canadian Bacon and Cheese Sandwiches to an Oriental steak sandwich dinner. Almost all the food can be prepared ahead and we have given special attention to the budget-conscious host. Here are feasts to suit every taste and occasion that will be just as much fun for the hosts as they are for the guests.

▸ A Note About Nutrition and Sandwiches

Until very recently Americans generally felt that giving up bread was a sound way to cut calories. However, scientific research has shown that grain products should make up a large share of our daily diet; the foods that we should cut back on to reduce calories are fats and refined sugars. It's now recognized that bread made from wholesome, basic ingredients is good for you. Most nonsweet yeast breads provide about 75 calories per ½-inch slice, and they supply valuable complex carbohydrates, vitamins, and minerals. The whole grain loaves provide needed fiber. So sandwiches not only offer great taste and ease of preparation, they make sense nutritionally as well.

Very often when sandwiches have a high calorie count it is the spreads and fillings that are the culprits. If you use lavish amounts of butter or margarine, which have 100 calories per tablespoon, you can easily reach mammoth calorie counts. Peanut butter, with 93 calories per tablespoon, runs a close second. One way to avoid this problem is simply to use smaller amounts of such spreads, but another possibility is to combine them with lower calorie extenders—combine mayonnaise with sour cream, which has only 30 calories per tablespoon, or with skim milk yogurt, which has only 7. In some sandwiches a good alternative to butter might be cream cheese (especially the whipped kind), which has about half the calories of butter and more nutritive value. You can lighten peanut butter with yogurt, orange juice, or pineapple juice. Some newer recipes call for honey to be blended with peanut butter, which is delicious but does not reduce the calorie count very much.

Cheeses other than cottage cheese and farmer cheese can be substantial sources of calories if you use thick slices. You can add the delicious flavor and richness of cheese by using a hand grater to aid in distributing a small amount of cheese evenly over bread.

▶ Brown-Bagging It

Often people think of brown-bagging as an economy measure rather than as a wonderful opportunity to guarantee just the lunch they want. If you've been thinking of portable lunches as limited in scope and time-consuming to prepare, this book will introduce you to a whole new approach to lunches-to-go that will make carrying your lunch to work or school a positive pleasure. All it takes is a little planning and a few pieces of easily affordable equipment to ensure delightful lunches from home day after day.

Of course taking your lunch to work does save money, but it also gives you the lunch you want when you want it—if you plan properly. And you have the extra bonus of lunch-hour time to attend yoga class, visit a museum, run an errand. No more waiting in line for an overpriced, not very interesting sandwich.

Use a bit of your weekend time for planning a bounty of tasty lunches for every day of the week. Write down the sandwiches you want, the accompaniments, and whatever plastic containers will allow you to tote vegetable garnishes, relishes, and drinks. You'll be amazed at how satisfying lunches from home can be. So happy brown-bagging!

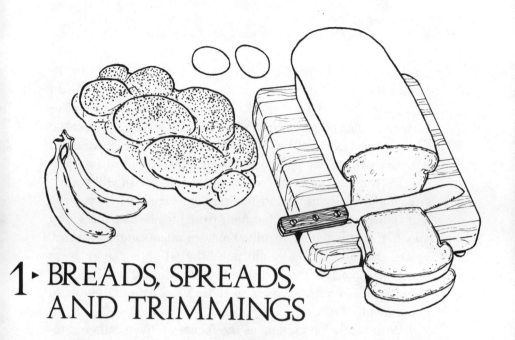

1▸ BREADS, SPREADS, AND TRIMMINGS

NO QUESTION ABOUT IT, YOU HAVE TO HAVE GOOD BREAD TO MAKE good sandwiches. You can start with a perfectly grilled hamburger, a memorable veal loaf, or a delectable chicken salad, but if the bread you put them on is limp and tasteless, the finished product is going to be a disappointment. The breads that make the best sandwiches taste delicious even in their unadorned state. And when you combine them with a first-rate filling you have outstanding fare. Happily, today's supermarkets offer an impressive variety of robust whole grain loaves, rich-tasting whites, sourdough specialties, seeded and unseeded rolls, and exotic pitas. With so many wonderful breads to choose from, the art of sandwich making can easily be raised to new heights.

Yet even though commercial bakers are turning out an array of excellent products, there is still a great deal to be said in favor of baking your own bread. Not only does it always seem to taste better, but most people get an immense satisfaction out of producing fragrant golden brown loaves from scratch. In addition, when you bake your own loaves, you can

1

create products tailored to your own needs. If you want salt-free or honey-sweetened breads, you can have them. You can substitute skim milk for whole. If you like, you can use oil or margarine instead of butter. When you make such changes the end products will not taste exactly the same as the originals, but they will still be delicious. Many substitutions are so simple that they do not even require a test run. These will be discussed more fully in "Bread-Baking Tips." However, if you decide to use a different kind of flour from the one called for, you may find that you have to adjust measurements and flavorings. Spices that add just the right note to a white loaf may seem bland when used with rye or whole wheat flour. The amount of liquid required may vary. So in those cases you may have to experiment a bit.

With sandwich making as the focus, we have gathered together a tempting collection of easy-to-follow kitchen-tested bread and roll recipes, including several quick breads for making special brunch and tea sandwiches. We've made a point to include several unusual yeast bread recipes—Sesame Whole Wheat Bread, Golden Cornmeal Yeast Bread, and Savory Cottage Cheese Bread—because part of the fun of home baking is turning out breads you don't find in the supermarket.

To add flavor and zest to meats, cheeses, and other fillings, we offer a varied collection of seasoned butters, a classic blender mayonnaise with delectable variations, and a yogurt dressing that is especially good on pita sandwiches.

We have shown cross-references to other recipes in the book with capitalized titles.

▸ Bread-Baking Tips

Before you start making bread, read through the recipe completely to make sure that you have the right ingredients and the correct pans, and also that you understand the steps required. Assemble everything you will need in one place—yeast, bowls, measuring cups and spoons, spices, flour, and so on. It makes the whole process much simpler and much more fun if you are well organized.

INGREDIENTS

Yeast. Yeast is a living plant that needs air, food, and moisture to grow. It grows best in a warm environment. Too much heat kills yeast; too little retards its growth. Yeast is sold in both dry and compressed cake form, but the dry form is much more widely available and we have listed that kind in our recipes. However, the two kinds can be used interchangeably—substitute a ¾-ounce cake of compressed yeast for every ¼-ounce package of active dry yeast. When you are combining yeast with water, use warm (105° F. to 115° F.) with dry yeast and lukewarm (80° F. to 90° F.) with the compressed variety. Warm water feels comfortably warm when tested on the inside of your wrist, and lukewarm almost cool.

Flour. All-purpose flour, a white flour that is half hard wheat flour and half soft wheat flour, is used in all of these recipes—sometimes alone, sometimes in combination with rye flour, whole wheat flour, or oats. Hard wheat flour provides a high gluten content for tensile strength, while soft wheat flour has a richer wheat flavor. You do not have to sift before measuring flour. Simply spoon it into a cup and level it off with a knife. Transfer to a bowl or a sheet of aluminum foil the full amount called for in the recipe. In recipes that require kneading, save ½ cup flour to sprinkle over bread board and to flour your hands. Flours vary in the amount of liquid they will absorb, so you may have to add a bit more flour to a recipe to achieve a dough that has the consistency called for.

Fats and Oils. Butter and margarine can be used interchangeably measure for measure. Cooking oil should be substituted for butter or margarine by measuring a scant spoonful of oil for each spoonful of butter or margarine.

Sugar, Honey, and Molasses. These ingredients can be interchanged in equal amounts, but you may have to decrease the other liquid in a recipe somewhat when you use honey or molasses in place of sugar. Because molasses imparts a stronger flavor than either sugar or honey, if you want to use it in a recipe that calls for as much as a half cup of honey or sugar, you might find that a smaller amount of molasses (⅓ or even ¼ cup) is enough.

Eggs. All eggs used in these recipes are large eggs.

TECHNIQUES

Glazes. Brush egg glazes or water on loaves of bread 10 to 20 minutes before removing from the oven and on rolls before baking.

For a shiny surface, brush with egg white that has been blended with 1 teaspoon of water.

For a shiny extra-brown surface, brush with a whole egg that has been blended with 1 teaspoon water.

For an extra-crisp crust, brush loaves with water.

Kneading. Turn dough out onto a lightly floured surface, preferably a bread board you reserve for this purpose. Rub a little flour on your hands. Push the dough mass with the heels of your hands, then fold the dough in half and give it a quarter turn. Repeat this pushing, folding, turning process until dough is smooth and elastic.

Some heavy-duty mixers come equipped with a dough hook for kneading bread. If you are using a mixer, be careful to follow manufacturer's directions. Knead for 3 to 4 minutes at low speed.

Rising. Bowl may be greased with butter, margarine, or oil. After patting dough into a ball, place it in a bowl and turn it to be sure all surfaces, especially the exposed top, are greased.

Always cover bowl or loaves with a slightly damp kitchen towel.

Doughs need an even temperature of 80° F. to 85° F. for rising. There are several common ways to provide a warm place for rising: .

1. Set bowl on rack in an unheated oven with a large pan of hot water on another rack beneath it.
2. Fill a large pan two-thirds full of boiling water, put a wire rack on top, and set bowl on it.
3. Set bowl in a deep pan of warm, not hot, water.
4. Put bowl in a draft-free place near, not on, range or radiator.

Testing for Doubled in Bulk. Press tips of two fingers lightly and quickly ½ inch into dough. If dent remains, dough is doubled.

Baking. When baking bread in glass loaf pans, use an oven temperature 25° less than specified in recipes. This prevents formation of a too-thick crust. Fully baked bread, unless otherwise noted, should sound hollow when bottom and sides are tapped with fingers.

Cooling. Remove from pans or baking sheet and put loaves on wire cake racks. Cover with kitchen towel for soft crust and leave uncovered for crisp crust.

Storing. Yeast bread kept at room temperature gets dry in two or three days. It keeps at least a week in the refrigerator. For best flavor serve at room temperature or toasted.

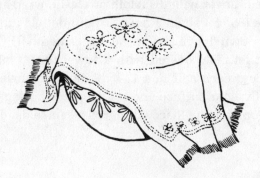

▸Yeast Breads

White Wheat Germ Bread
MAKES 2 LOAVES

A firm-textured, rich-tasting sandwich bread that is lightly flecked with wheat germ to add more flavor and nutrition.

2 cups milk
¼ cup (½ stick) butter or margarine
2 tablespoons honey
2 teaspoons salt
¼ cup warm water (105° F. to 115° F.)
1 package active dry yeast
6 cups all-purpose flour
½ cup wheat germ

In saucepan heat milk, butter or margarine, and honey until very warm. Butter will not be melted completely. Stir in salt. Place warm water in a large bowl and sprinkle yeast over it. Let stand for 5 minutes. When milk mixture is lukewarm, combine it with yeast mixture. Stir in 3 cups of flour 1 cup at a time. Stir with a spoon and add wheat germ and 2½ cups more flour, or enough so that dough comes away from the sides of bowl. Turn out on lightly floured surface. Knead for 8 to 10 minutes, adding ½ cup more flour as necessary to produce smooth, elastic dough. Dough will appear to be blistered beneath the surface. Place in a large greased bowl, turning to be sure top is fully greased. Cover with dishcloth or plastic wrap and set in a warm place (85° F.) about 1 hour or until doubled in bulk.

Punch down dough and knead until smooth. Divide dough in half and let rest covered with a towel for 10 minutes. To shape, roll out each half in a 12-by-9-inch rectangle. If dough sticks, lightly flour surface and rolling pin. Starting at narrow edge, roll up dough. Place each roll seam side down in a greased 9-by-5-by-3-inch loaf pan. Cover with towel and let rise until doubled, about 45 minutes. Place loaves in a 400° F. oven and bake for about 35 minutes or until loaves sound hollow when tapped on the bottom. Remove from pans and cool on racks.

Crusty Italian Bread
MAKES 2 LARGE OR 8 INDIVIDUAL LOAVES

A simple bread—just flour, water, yeast, and salt—that is simply delicious. Try it with meatballs, Olive Meat Loaf, prosciutto, or eggplant parmigiano.

2 packages active dry yeast
2½ cups warm water (105° F. to 115° F.)
1 tablespoon salt
7 to 7½ cups all-purpose flour
1 egg white, beaten with 1 teaspoon water
Cornmeal

In a large mixing bowl, sprinkle yeast on warm water. Stir to mix thoroughly. Add salt and 2 cups flour; stir to blend. Stir in 4 more cups flour, 1 cup at a time, blending thoroughly. Knead in 1 more cup flour, or a bit more, to make a stiff dough. Turn out onto a lightly floured surface and knead for approximately 15 minutes until dough is smooth and elastic. Place dough in lightly greased bowl, turning to make sure top is greased. Cover with plastic wrap or a dish towel and set in a warm place to rise until doubled in bulk, about 1½ hours. Punch down and let double again, about 1 hour.

Turn dough out onto lightly floured surface, divide it in half with sharp knife, and form each half into a ball. Cover and let rest for 10 minutes. Dough may be shaped into two large round loaves, scored across the top with a sharp knife (make four parallel cuts and four crossways cuts), or eight small round loaves, scored with a cross on the top. Brush loaves with egg white and water mixture. Sprinkle cornmeal on cookie sheet and place loaves on sheet. Let rise uncovered until a little less than doubled in bulk. Place a small pan of boiling water on the lowest rack or floor of the oven to ensure crisp crust. Bake large loaves in 375° F. oven for 40 to 45 minutes or until golden brown. Bake small loaves in 400° F. oven for 20 to 25 minutes. Remove loaves from oven and place on wire rack to cool.

Challah
MAKES 2 LOAVES

Light in texture and golden in color, this is the traditional Jewish Sabbath bread. It is usually braided and flecked with poppy seeds, but you can also bake it unseeded in loaf pans. While it is rich, it is not sweet—and it makes wonderful sandwiches.

> 1 package active dry yeast
> 2 tablespoons sugar
> 1½ cups warm water (105° F. to 115° F.)
> About 5 cups all-purpose flour
> 2 teaspoons salt
> 2 eggs
> 2 tablespoons vegetable oil
> 1 egg yolk, slightly beaten
> 2 tablespoons poppy seeds

Combine yeast, sugar, and ¼ cup warm water. Let stand 5 minutes. Measure 4½ cups flour and salt into a large bowl. Make a well in center of flour and drop in eggs, oil, remaining 1¼ cups warm water, and yeast mixture. Work liquids into flour. Transfer to floured board and knead until dough is smooth and elastic, working in enough of remaining flour to make a manageable dough. Place in oiled bowl, cover with damp kitchen towel and let stand in warm place until doubled in bulk, about 1 hour.

Punch dough down and divide it into six equal parts. Between lightly floured hands roll dough into six strips of equal length. Braid three strips to make each loaf and place on oiled baking sheet about 6 inches apart. Cover and let rise until doubled. Brush with egg yolk and sprinkle with poppy seeds. Bake in 375° F. oven 45 to 50 minutes, or until golden brown. Cool on rack.

Pita (Pocket Bread)
MAKES 8 LOAVES

These Middle Eastern flat breads are ideal for sandwiches. Just cut them in half or cut off a sliver at the top of a whole pita, gently separate the two sides, and fill with sliced meat, cheese, salads, shredded vegetables, sprouts. These seem to inspire sandwich-making creativity. Serve them at barbecues, sandwich buffets, and the easiest picnics ever.

1 package active dry yeast
1¼ cups warm water (105° F. to 115° F.)
¼ teaspoon sugar
1½ teaspoons salt
1½ tablespoons olive oil
3 cups all-purpose flour

In a large warm bowl sprinkle yeast into warm water and let stand for 5 minutes. Stir to dissolve. Add sugar, salt, oil, and flour. Mix and knead until smooth and elastic, about 10 minutes. Place in greased bowl, turning to grease top. Cover and let rise in warm place until doubled in bulk, about 1 hour and 15 minutes.

Punch dough down, divide in eight equal pieces, and shape into balls. On lightly floured surface roll out each ball in 6-inch circle; place on greased 7-inch square of foil. Let rise in warm place about 1 hour. Bake on lowest rack in preheated 500° F.

oven about 7 minutes or until puffed and lightly browned. Serve at once or store, cooled, in plastic bags.

Savory Cottage Cheese Bread
MAKES 1 LOAF

Cottage cheese gives this loaf a moist crumb, and the onion and herb add piquant keynotes. We like this best with Swiss cheese, ham salad, curried egg salad, or a splendid combination of chive-flavored cream cheese, cucumber, and tomato.

    2 teaspoons instant minced onion
    1 package active dry yeast
    ¼ cup warm water (105° F. to 115° F.)
    1 tablespoon butter or margarine, softened
    1 teaspoon salt
    1 teaspoon marjoram
    1 cup (8 ounces) small-curd creamed cottage cheese, at
        room temperature
    2 tablespoons sugar
    ¼ teaspoon baking soda
    1 egg
    2 to 2½ cups all-purpose flour

Add a small amount (about 2 tablespoons) of water to onion and let stand for 5 minutes. Drain if necessary. Soften yeast in ¼ cup water. In medium bowl combine onion, butter or margarine, salt, marjoram, cottage cheese, sugar, baking soda, and egg. Stir to mix thoroughly. Add yeast and blend thoroughly. Gradually add enough flour to make a firm dough. Turn out onto a lightly floured surface and knead for about 5 minutes, until dough is smooth. Shape into a loaf and put in a buttered 9-by-5-by-3-inch loaf pan. Let rise until doubled in bulk, 40 to 45 minutes. Bake in a 375° F. oven until done, approximately 40 minutes. Cool on rack before slicing.

Buttermilk Cheese Bread

MAKES 2 LOAVES

An ideal sandwich bread with a rich Cheddar flavor. Try it with thinly sliced ham and watercress, sliced turkey and romaine lettuce, or bacon, Boston lettuce, and tomato.

1 cup buttermilk
1 cup water
⅓ cup butter
¼ cup sugar
2½ teaspoons salt
1 package active dry yeast
½ teaspoon baking soda
1½ cups shredded sharp Cheddar cheese
5 to 5½ cups all-purpose flour

Heat buttermilk and water with the butter until butter melts. Stir in sugar and salt and cool to about 120° F. (warm). In a large bowl of electric mixer combine yeast, baking soda, and shredded cheese with 2 cups flour. Add buttermilk mixture and beat at low speed 30 seconds, then beat at medium-high speed 3 minutes. With wooden spoon, stir in enough additional flour to make a soft but firm dough (3 to 3½ cups). Turn out onto floured board. Knead 7 to 10 minutes, or until smooth and elastic. Put in greased bowl and turn greased side up. Cover and let rise in warm place until doubled in bulk, about 1 hour. Punch down and shape in two loaves. Put in greased 9-by-5-by-3-inch loaf pans and let rise until doubled, about 30 to 40 minutes. Bake at 400° F. for 30 to 40 minutes. Turn out and cool on cake racks before cutting.

Buttermilk Raisin Bread
MAKES 2 LOAVES

Golden raisins stud this light and slightly sweet tea bread. Just spread it with peanut butter or top it with ham or sliced tongue or cumin-flavored chicken salad, and you'll see why it's one of our all-time favorites.

    1 package active dry yeast
    ¼ cup warm water (105° F. to 115° F.)
    1½ cups buttermilk, at room temperature
    ⅓ cup butter or margarine, softened
    1½ teaspoons salt
    ⅓ cup sugar
    1 teaspoon baking soda
    1 cup golden raisins
    2 eggs
    5 to 5½ cups all-purpose flour

Sprinkle yeast on warm water and let stand 5 minutes. Heat buttermilk, butter or margarine, salt, and sugar until butter is melted. Cool to lukewarm. In a large bowl combine yeast and buttermilk mixture; add baking soda, raisins, eggs, and 2 cups flour. Beat vigorously until blended. Gradually add more flour to make a dough that is firm but not too stiff. Turn out onto floured board and knead until smooth and satiny. Put in greased bowl and turn to grease top. Cover and let stand in warm place 1½ hours or until doubled in bulk. Punch down and shape into two loaves. Put in two greased 9-by-5-by-3-inch loaf pans. Let rise again 1 hour. Bake in 350° F. oven 45 minutes, or until done. Turn out on cake rack. Cool before cutting.

Golden Cornmeal Yeast Bread
MAKES 2 LOAVES

A slightly sweet loaf with a hint of crunchiness in the texture, this bread seems created to make ham sandwiches, old-fashioned ham salad sandwiches, and fiesta egg salad (flavored with cumin and green chilies) sandwiches.

1 package active dry yeast
¼ cup warm water (105° F. to 115° F.)
⅓ cup sugar
⅓ cup butter or margarine
1 tablespoon salt
2 cups milk
About 7 cups all-purpose flour
2 eggs, well beaten
1 cup yellow cornmeal

In a small bowl, dissolve yeast in the warm water. Put sugar, butter or margarine, and salt in large mixing bowl. Scald milk (heat it to just below a boil), pour over sugar-butter mixture, and stir to mix well. Let stand until lukewarm, then add yeast, 4 cups flour, eggs, and cornmeal, and beat with a wooden spoon until smooth. Stir in enough additional flour to make a soft but firm dough. Turn out onto floured surface and knead 5 minutes, or until dough is smooth and satiny and does not stick to board. Grease bowl and add dough, turning greased side up. Cover and let rise in warm place 1 hour, or until doubled in bulk.

Punch dough down and let rise 10 minutes longer. Shape in two loaves and put in well-greased 9-by-5-by-3-inch loaf pans. Let rise 35 minutes, or until it reaches top of pan. Bake in preheated 350° F. oven 50 minutes, or until loaves sound hollow when tapped with knuckle. Turn out on wire racks and let stand until cold.

Honey Oatmeal Bread
MAKES 2 LOAVES

Oats give this loaf firm texture and a delicate nutty flavor. It goes well with ham, cheese, chicken, or lettuce and tomatoes. Or try a festive combination of sliced turkey, cranberry sauce, and romaine lettuce on this lovely bread.

1 cup quick-cooking (not instant) rolled oats
2 cups milk, heated to just boiling
1 package active dry yeast
½ cup warm water (105° F. to 115° F.)
2 tablespoons butter or margarine, softened
¼ cup clover honey, or other pale honey
2 teaspoons salt
½ teaspoon ground ginger
4 to 4½ cups all-purpose flour

Put oats in a large bowl and pour hot milk over them. Stir and let stand until lukewarm (about 30 minutes). Sprinkle yeast on the warm water. Let stand 5 minutes, then stir to dissolve. Add the yeast mixture, butter or margarine, honey, salt, and ginger to the oat mixture. Stir in flour, ½ cup at a time, mixing well. (Reserve last ½ cup flour for kneading.) Turn out onto floured work surface and knead 8 to 10 minutes until dough is smooth and satiny, adding flour as necessary. Place dough in greased bowl, turning to make sure top is greased, and set in warm place until dough has doubled in bulk, about 1 hour.

Punch dough down and divide in half. Knead for a few seconds to remove air bubbles. Shape into two loaves and place in greased 9-by-5-by-3-inch loaf pans. Let rise until almost doubled, about 45 minutes. Bake in preheated 350° F. oven for 45 to 50 minutes. Cool on rack.

Sesame Whole Wheat Bread
MAKES 3 LOAVES

A robust loaf with a rich wheat flavor that stands up well to robust cheeses such as aged Cheddar, Gorgonzola, or Camembert; salami; Italian meat loaf; or liverwurst.

    1 package active dry yeast
    3 cups warm water (105° F. to 115° F.)
    2 tablespoons honey
    2 teaspoons salt
    2 eggs
    ¼ cup safflower oil
    1 cup nonfat dry milk powder
    ½ cup wheat germ
    ¼ cup sesame seeds
    3 cups whole wheat flour
    4 to 4½ cups all-purpose flour

Sprinkle yeast on water. Let stand for a few minutes, then stir until dissolved. Add honey, salt, eggs, oil, dry milk, wheat germ, and sesame seeds; beat hard for 2 minutes. Stir in flours, reserving ½ cup all-purpose flour for kneading. Turn out onto a floured surface and knead until smooth and satiny. Put in greased bowl; turn once and cover with plastic wrap. Let rise in warm place until doubled in bulk, about 1 hour.

Punch dough down and let rise for about 30 minutes. Shape into three loaves and put in three greased loaf pans (9 by 5 by 3 inches). Let rise until doubled, about 1 hour. Bake in preheated 350° F. oven for about 45 minutes. When loaves are done bottom will sound hollow when tapped with knuckles. Turn out on rack to cool.

Whole Wheat Walnut Raisin Bread
MAKES 2 LOAVES

A hearty, full-flavored loaf that makes wonderful sandwiches, either plain or toasted. For a surprise breakfast, serve it with a layer of peanut butter and thinly sliced banana. Or try it with chicken salad studded with grapes.

    4 to 5 cups all-purpose flour
    2 cups whole wheat flour
    1 package active dry yeast
    1 tablespoon salt
    1¾ cups milk
    ¼ cup butter or margarine
    ⅓ cup honey
    2 eggs
    1 teaspoon cinnamon
    1 cup seedless raisins
    1 cup chopped walnuts

In large bowl of electric mixer stir together 1 cup all-purpose flour and 1 cup whole wheat flour. Add yeast and salt. In saucepan heat milk, butter or margarine, and honey over low heat until very warm (120° F. to 130° F.). Gradually stir milk-honey mixture into flour mixture and beat at medium speed 2 minutes, scraping bowl occasionally. Add eggs and remaining cup of whole wheat flour; beat at high speed 2 minutes. Stir in cinnamon, raisins, and nuts. Add enough of remaining all-purpose flour to make a soft dough. Turn out on a lightly floured surface and knead 8 to 10 minutes, adding small amounts of flour if dough remains sticky, until dough is smooth and elastic. Shape into ball and put in greased bowl, turning to grease top. Cover with plastic wrap or clean dish towel and let rise in a warm place until doubled in bulk, about 1½ hours.

Punch dough down, cover with a damp towel, and let rest for 10 minutes. Divide dough in half and with rolling pin lightly roll out each half to a 14-by-9-inch rectangle. Beginning at narrow end, roll up each as for jelly roll. Tuck ends under and put each roll, seam side down, in a greased 9-by-5-by-3-inch pan. Cover lightly with towel and let rise in warm place until doubled in bulk, about 1½ hours. Bake in preheated 375° F. oven 35 to 40 minutes, or until loaves sound hollow when lightly tapped with fingers. Cool in pans 10 minutes, then turn loaves out on rack to cool.

Seeded Whole Wheat Sandwich Buns
MAKES 12 BUNS

These savory whole grain buns are an ideal match for grilled burgers, but try them, too, with a good-quality Swiss cheese and Boston lettuce or a robust Genoa salami and tangy mustard.

½ cup milk
¼ cup (½ stick) butter or margarine
3 tablespoons honey
1 teaspoon salt
¼ cup warm water (105° F. to 115° F.)
1 package active dry yeast
2½ cups whole wheat flour
2 cups all-purpose flour
1 egg white, beaten with 2 tablespoons water
About 2 tablespoons sesame seeds

In a saucepan heat milk, butter or margarine, honey, and salt until very warm. Butter will not be melted completely. Place warm water in large bowl, add yeast and stir to blend. Let stand 5 minutes. When milk mixture is lukewarm, combine it with yeast mixture. Stir in whole wheat flour and 1½ cups all-purpose flour (set aside ½ cup to add when kneading), ½ cup at a time, stirring after each addition until a stiff dough is formed. Turn out onto lightly floured surface. Knead for 8 to 10 minutes, adding ½ cup all-purpose flour as necessary to produce smooth, elastic dough. Dough will appear to be blistered just beneath the surface. Place in large greased bowl, turning to grease entire surface. Cover bowl with dishcloth and let rise in warm, draft-free area until doubled in bulk.

Punch down dough and knead until smooth. Divide into twelve equal portions. Roll each portion into a ball between palms and place on greased baking sheets about 2 inches apart. Press down each ball to flatten, cover, and let rise for 30 minutes. Brush lightly with beaten egg white and sprinkle with sesame seeds. Preheat oven to 375° F. Bake until golden brown, about 18 to 20 minutes. Cover with dish towels and cool on racks.

Finnish-Style Health Bread
MAKES 2 LOAVES

The Finns make some of the best breads in the world—dark full-flavored loaves that are perfect for sandwiches. This one combines rye and wheat flours, plus a liberal measure of wheat germ.

2¼ cups buttermilk
1 package active dry yeast
¼ cup warm water (105° F. to 115° F.)
1 teaspoon salt
1¼ cups rye flour
1¼ cups whole wheat flour
Wheat germ
2 cups all-purpose flour

In a saucepan, heat buttermilk to lukewarm. Dissolve the yeast in the warm water in a mixing bowl. Add buttermilk, salt, and rye and wheat flours together with ¼ cup wheat germ, and stir with a wooden spoon until well blended. Gradually add the all-purpose flour, beating until smooth. Turn out onto a floured board and knead until smooth and elastic. Cover loosely and let rest on the board 30 minutes. Divide the dough in half and pat each piece into a round cake 6 inches in diameter. Brush with water and press the tops into some wheat germ. Put on a lightly greased baking sheet. Let rise 1 hour or until doubled in bulk. Cut a crisscross pattern on the tops with a very sharp knife. Bake in a preheated 400° F. oven for 30 minutes, or until done. Cool on rack.

Sour Rye Bread

MAKES 3 LOAVES

A coarse bread with a fermented flavor, this tangy rye is great with Westphalian ham, Jarlsberg cheese, or garlicky sausage. Note that you start it the day before baking it.

    2 packages active dry yeast
    3½ cups warm water (115° F. to 120° F.)
    8 cups whole rye flour
    ¼ cup molasses
    1 tablespoon salt
    1 tablespoon cumin seeds, lightly crushed, or 1 tablespoon
        caraway seeds
    3½ to 4 cups all-purpose flour

In large mixing bowl, sprinkle yeast on water, let soften, and stir to dissolve. Gradually stir in rye flour. Cover dough with a damp towel and let rise at room temperature overnight.

Next day, punch down the dough, add molasses, salt, cumin or caraway seeds, and about 1 cup all-purpose flour, and mix well. Gradually stir in more flour until a stiff dough is formed. Turn out onto floured surface and knead until smooth and elastic and dough no longer sticks to hands. Divide into three equal pieces and shape each in a smooth loaf about 12 inches long. Put on greased large baking sheet and let rise in warm draft-free place for 35 to 40 minutes, or until a few cracks develop in tops of loaves. Bake in preheated 350° F. oven 1 hour, or until bread is done. Brush loaves with hot water, once toward end of baking time and again just before putting on rack to cool; then cover with several towels.

▸ Quick Breads for Tea Sandwiches

Easy to make and delicious to eat, these flavorful breads are ideal for making tea or party sandwiches. Both cream cheese and cottage cheese combined with fruits and nuts are popular fillings for sandwiches made with these treats. Other possibilities might be nut butters that have been lightened with fruit juice or yogurt, jams, and plain butter or margarine. But do try baked beans on the Baked Applesauce Brown Bread, and thinly sliced ham and peanut butter on the Honey-Nut Quick Bread.

Buttermilk Pecan Bread
MAKES 1 LOAF

⅓ cup butter or margarine, softened
½ cup sugar
1 egg
2 cups all-purpose flour
1 teaspoon salt
2 teaspoons double-acting baking powder
¼ teaspoon baking soda
¾ cup chopped pecans
1¼ cups buttermilk

In a large mixing bowl, cream together butter or margarine and sugar until light and fluffy. Beat in egg. Combine dry ingredients, including nuts, separately. Add flour-nut mixture to first mixture alternately with buttermilk, beating after each addition. Put in greased 9-by-5-by-3-inch loaf pan lined on the bottom with waxed paper. Bake in preheated 325° F. oven 1 to 1¼ hours. Turn out gently on cake rack, and allow to cool thoroughly before cutting.

Orange-Nut Bread
MAKES 1 LOAF

2½ cups all-purpose flour
3 teaspoons double-acting baking powder
1 cup sugar
1 teaspoon salt
¼ cup vegetable shortening
1 egg
¾ cup milk
¼ cup orange juice
3 tablespoons grated orange rind
1 cup chopped walnuts or pecans

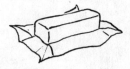

Combine flour, baking powder, sugar, and salt in bowl and stir with fork to mix. Cut in shortening with pastry blender or fork. Beat egg slightly with fork and stir in milk, orange juice, and orange rind. Add to dry ingredients, stirring only enough to moisten. Gently stir in nuts. Pour into greased 9-by-5-by-3-inch loaf pan, spreading to corners and leaving a slight depression in center. Let stand 20 minutes. Bake in preheated 350° F. oven 55 to 60 minutes. Let stand 5 minutes, then turn out on rack to cool. Wrap and store overnight before slicing.

Baked Applesauce Brown Bread
MAKES 1 LOAF

2 cups whole wheat flour
1 cup stone-ground yellow cornmeal
¾ teaspoon salt
1 teaspoon baking soda
1 cup buttermilk
1 cup unsulfured molasses
¾ cup canned applesauce
¾ cup seedless raisins

Mix flour, cornmeal, salt, and baking soda in a bowl. Add buttermilk and molasses and beat with a spoon until smooth. Fold in applesauce and raisins and spread in greased 9-by-5-by-3-inch loaf pan. Bake in preheated 350° F. oven for 35 to 40 minutes, or until a toothpick inserted in bread comes out clean. Cool on rack before slicing.

Honey-Nut Quick Bread

MAKES 1 LOAF

2 tablespoons butter or margarine, softened
⅓ cup honey
3 tablespoons sugar
2 eggs
⅔ cup whole wheat flour
1 cup all-purpose flour
1½ teaspoons baking powder
½ teaspoon salt
½ teaspoon baking soda
½ cup buttermilk
½ cup pitted dates, chopped
½ cup chopped nuts
1 teaspoon grated lemon rind

Cream butter or margarine, honey, and sugar thoroughly. Add eggs one at a time, beating after each until blended. Add whole wheat flour. Combine all-purpose flour, baking powder, salt, and baking soda and add alternately with buttermilk, beating until blended. Add remaining ingredients and pour into greased 8½-by-4½-by-2½-inch glass loaf pan. Bake in preheated 325° F. oven about 50 minutes. Turn out on rack and cool thoroughly before slicing.

Best-Ever Banana Bread
MAKES 1 LOAF

⅓ cup butter or margarine
⅔ cup light brown sugar
2 eggs, slightly beaten
1¾ cups all-purpose flour
2 teaspoons baking powder
¼ teaspoon baking soda
1 cup mashed ripe bananas (2 or 3)
1 cup chopped walnuts or pecans
½ teaspoon salt

Cream together butter or margarine and sugar until light and fluffy. Add eggs and beat until thick and pale lemon in color. Combine dry ingredients and add alternately with bananas to butter-sugar mixture. Blend well after each addition. Line bottom of a greased 9-by-5-by-3-inch loaf pan with waxed paper and spoon in batter. Bake in preheated 350° F. oven for 1 hour. Let cool in pan for 20 minutes before turning out and cooling thoroughly on cake rack.

▸ Seasoned Butters

Butter—or margarine—that has been enriched with herbs, spices, and other flavorings can turn a simple sandwich into a memorable treat. And the good news is that these flavorful compound butters are very easy to make. Also, they inspire creativity. After you've tried your hand at several of our recipes, you'll find it is an easy matter to invent a few delightful combinations of your own. Why not add chopped strawberries, olives, or mushrooms, grated citrus rinds, ground ginger, peppers, chutney?

The simplest of our recipes are the herb butters, which are usually just a well-balanced combination of butter, lemon juice, and finely minced herb. But even the slightly more complex Scallion-Mustard Butter, Watercress Butter, and Anchovy-Dill Butter are a snap to make. If you and your family are dedicated sandwich lovers, you will probably want to make up one or two of these spreads to have on hand.

Generally speaking, it is best to use full-flavored or pungent butters with hearty meats and cheeses. For example, try Garlic Butter or Scallion-Mustard Butter with cold roast beef or lamb, meat loaf, provolone, blue cheese, or sapsago. Milder compounds such as Shrimp Butter would be just right for a sliced egg sandwich, sliced cucumbers, or a bland cheese. Try Watercress Butter on a Sour Rye Bread with ham and Swiss. Or Basil Butter with Cheddar, cold roast veal, or sliced turkey.

Basic Herb Butter

Quantity used for herb butters depends on the strength of the herb. If you are using dried herbs use about 1 to 1½ teaspoons herbs to 1 stick butter.

½ cup (1 stick) butter or margarine
1 tablespoon lemon juice
Salt to taste (if you are using unsalted butter)
Freshly ground black pepper to taste
1 to 2 tablespoons finely chopped fresh herbs, such as basil, parsley, dill, chervil, marjoram, thyme, or rosemary

Place butter or margarine in a small mixing bowl and cream it by smoothing and softening with the back of a large spoon against sides of bowl. Beat in lemon juice, salt, and pepper. Add herbs and blend thoroughly. Chilling for a few hours will help develop flavor, but serve at room temperature.

Garlic Butter. Add 1 teaspoon crushed or finely minced garlic to parsley-flavored Herb Butter.

Maître d'Hôtel Butter. Add 2 tablespoons finely chopped chives and ½ teaspoon Worcestershire sauce to parsley-flavored Herb Butter.

Scallion-Mustard Butter

½ cup (1 stick) butter or margarine
2 tablespoons finely chopped scallions, including some of
    the green part
1½ teaspoons Dijon mustard

Cream butter or margarine, add other ingredients, and beat to blend thoroughly.

Shrimp Butter

½ cup (1 stick) butter or margarine
4½-ounce can shrimps, drained and finely chopped
¼ teaspoon dried dillweed
2 teaspoons lemon juice
Freshly ground black pepper to taste

Cream butter or margarine, add other ingredients, and beat to blend thoroughly.

Watercress Butter

½ cup (1 stick) butter
2 teaspoons lemon juice
¼ teaspoon paprika
½ cup finely chopped watercress leaves
¼ teaspoon black pepper

Cream butter, add other ingredients, and beat to blend thoroughly. Chill for a few hours to develop flavor.

Anchovy-Dill Butter

½ cup (1 stick) butter
1 tablespoon lemon juice
1 teaspoon chopped fresh dill or ¼ teaspoon dried
2 teaspoons finely chopped chives or scallions
1 tablespoon anchovy paste

Cream butter, add other ingredients, and beat to blend thoroughly. Chill for a few hours to develop flavor.

Blender Mayonnaise
MAKES 1⅔ CUPS

If you have never tasted homemade mayonnaise, or you haven't made it for a long time, our simple blender version will introduce you to a new world of good eating. This velvety, golden-rich dressing, with its fresh taste of lemon, seems to have been created to make perfect lobster, shrimp, and chicken salad, to enhance a classic sliced turkey sandwich, and to add just the right grace note to a simple sweet onion sandwich on

White Wheat Germ Bread. Blend up a batch and see how it also transforms ordinary tuna and egg salad into company fare.

>1 egg or 2 egg yolks, at room temperature
>¼ teaspoon dry mustard or 1 teaspoon Dijon mustard
>½ teaspoon salt
>¼ teaspoon white pepper
>2 tablespoons lemon juice
>½ cup olive oil
>1 cup vegetable oil, preferably peanut or safflower

Put egg or yolks in blender container. Add mustard, salt, pepper, and lemon juice and blend for several seconds to mix ingredients thoroughly. With motor running at low speed, add oils very slowly in a fine, steady stream. As mixture thickens increase blender speed to high until all of both oils is added and texture is thick. Use a rubber spatula to transfer mayonnaise to a small bowl or screw-top jar. Serve immediately or refrigerate for up to 1 week in airtight container.

Garlic Mayonnaise. Add 1 medium clove garlic, crushed or pressed, to egg-lemon mixture in blender container before adding oils.

Green Mayonnaise. Chop 10 to 12 spinach leaves or 10 to 12 sprigs of watercress or mixture of both. Add these plus 1 tablespoon finely chopped parsley and ½ to 1 teaspoon tarragon to blender container after oils have been blended in. Blend for a few seconds to mix thoroughly and turn out into bowl. If green mayonnaise is going to be kept for several days, it is desirable to blanch spinach and watercress for 1 minute in boiling water and then chop. This blanching will help to retain bright green color and fresh flavor.

Herb Mayonnaise. Stir 1 or 2 tablespoons finely chopped chives, tarragon, dill, chervil, or Italian parsley into 1 cup mayonnaise.

Green Peppercorn Mayonnaise. Stir 1 tablespoon green peppercorns and 1 tablespoon finely chopped chives or small scallions into 1 cup mayonnaise.

Curried Mayonnaise. Stir 1 to 2½ teaspoons curry powder into
1 cup mayonnaise.

Mustard Mayonnaise. Stir 2 teaspoons Dijon or other fine prepared mustard into 1 cup mayonnaise.

Horseradish Mayonnaise. Stir 1 tablespoon prepared horseradish and 1 tablespoon finely chopped parsley into 1 cup mayonnaise.

Pimiento Mayonnaise. Purée 2 chopped canned pimientos in
blender and add to 1 cup mayonnaise. Stir in finely minced
chives or parsley and blend thoroughly.

Russian Dressing. Add 3 or 4 tablespoons catsup or chili sauce,
1 tablespoon prepared horseradish, 1 or 2 teaspoons finely
chopped onion, and a dash of Worcestershire sauce to 1 cup
mayonnaise.

Tartar Sauce. Mince 1½ to 2 tablespoons sour pickles and 1 tablespoon capers, drain on a paper towel, and stir into 1 cup
mayonnaise. Add 1 tablespoon each minced tarragon and
parsley and blend thoroughly.

Yogurt Dressing
MAKES 1¼ CUPS

1 cup plain yogurt
2 teaspoons lemon juice
1 small clove garlic
2 scallions, chopped fine
1 tablespoon chopped parsley
Salt and freshly ground black pepper to taste
2 tablespoons toasted sesame seeds (optional)

Put ¼ cup yogurt, lemon juice, and garlic in a blender and blend for several seconds. In a small bowl combine remaining yogurt with garlic mixture, add scallions, parsley, and seasonings, and stir to blend thoroughly. Add sesame seeds if you like. Especially good on pita bread sandwiches.

▸ Trimmings

Vegetable garnishes—lettuce, tomatoes, cress, sliced cucumber, shredded carrots, or cabbage—not only add flavor and texture to sandwiches, they provide additional nutritional benefits. Also, because they are lower in calories than such fillings as meat, cheese, and eggs, they serve as valuable extenders.

Another flavor and texture note now frequently added to sandwiches consists of a light sprinkling of seeds or chopped nuts. These additions also increase nutritive value. A tablespoon of sesame seeds is 55 calories, while the same amount of sunflower seeds is 44 calories. Walnuts are 33 calories per tablespoon, and pecans are a bit more.

2 ▸ LUNCHBOX AND PICNIC FAVORITES: HEARTY COLD SANDWICHES

BECAUSE PICNICS SPELL ADVENTURE TO US—INTERESTING FOOD IN an exciting new setting—we like to think of every lunchtime as an opportunity for a picnic. It makes us explore new recipes and new combinations. And there are so many delectable possibilities to choose from. No need to repeat yourself and have an ordinary lunch.

To start you off on a course of adventurous eating, we have gathered together a bountiful selection of best-ever recipes for cold sandwiches. Heading our list are delightful cold roast beef suggestions, unusual ham sandwiches, splendid chicken and turkey ideas, and some of the best meat loaves we've ever tasted. Obviously we've included tuna salad, egg salad, shrimp and salmon salads, cheeses of all kinds, vegetable delights, and some truly remarkable peanut butter combinations. For portable feasts (both brown-bag lunches and festive picnics) as well as lunches in your own home, there are sandwiches to suit every taste and every budget.

Wonderful lunches take a bit of planning. A few minutes of thought and effort each weekend can pay great dividends all through the week. Read through the recipes that strike your fancy, decide which ones you'd like to try, and then write down a plan. If you love meat loaf sandwiches, bake a slightly larger than usual one for dinner so that you'll have enough left over for lunch. If you like sliced egg or egg salad sandwiches, hard-cook a few eggs while you're preparing dinner the night before. If sliced chicken and watercress sandwiches make you feel pampered, by all means poach a chicken breast—it takes only minutes—and treat yourself to a noontime indulgence. Armed with this book and a master plan, you will find that it is easy to create lunches that offer a welcome respite in the middle of your busy days.

▸ Cooking Tips

Once you've made a plan for your weekly lunches you're way ahead of the game, but it also helps to keep certain cooking tips in mind. Wash and drain lettuce and other greens the night before—while you're making salad for dinner. Follow a tested method for hard-cooking eggs so that whites will be firm but tender and yellows cooked through and without a tinge of gray. If you use a seasoned broth to poach chicken breasts, your sliced chicken will be more flavorful as well as moist. And to make meat loaves more interesting, experiment with new herbs and spices.

HOW TO HARD-COOK EGGS PERFECTLY
First warm the eggs in warm water from the tap or prick the large end with a pin to make sure the shell will not crack in the boiling water. Next, with a slotted spoon slowly lower the eggs into enough boiling water to cover. When the water returns to a boil, lower the heat to just boiling and time the eggs for 12 minutes (this assumes you will be using large eggs, as we do

throughout the book). As soon as the time limit is up, pour off the boiling water and add cold tap water to the pan. This quick cooling prevents discoloration of the yolk. Refrigerate to cool thoroughly and then peel.

POACHING CHICKEN FOR SANDWICHES

You can make delicious chicken salad from leftover roast or broiled chicken, but the very best sliced chicken sandwiches are made from poached chicken breasts that have been simmered in broth until just tender. This is also true of turkey sandwiches, and since you can now buy turkey breasts and halves separately, you can make delectable sliced turkey sandwiches for a crowd.

Wash the poultry breasts and put them in a heavy saucepan with water to cover. Add 1 onion stuck with a clove, 1 rib celery, a bay leaf, thyme, parsley, and 2 or 3 peppercorns. Use 1 teaspoon of salt for each quart of water. Bring the water to a boil, lower to a simmer, and cook the breasts for 10 to 12 minutes—exact timing will depend on the size of the breast. Obviously a turkey breast will take much longer, and since turkey breasts vary so much in size, times will vary. When meat is opaque and white throughout, the breast is done. Remove breasts from broth and reserve broth for soup making. Cover breasts with plastic wrap and refrigerate until completely cool before slicing.

SEASONING MEAT LOAVES FOR COLD SANDWICHES

Well-seasoned meat loaves—beef, veal, pork, and ham—make delicious sandwiches. One of their great appeals is that you can vary seasonings and other flavorings to suit your own taste. But do remember that seasonings are less pronounced in cold meat loaf than in hot, so be generous when you are adding pepper, grated onion, or herbs.

▸ A Note on Pita Sandwiches

Throughout the Middle East pita is served both at mealtimes and for snacks and picnics to hold grilled meats, spicy chicken, and vegetable salads. These handy pocket breads are ideal when you want to serve such combinations as thinly sliced mozzarella, vine-ripened tomatoes, and fresh basil; thinly sliced ham wrapped around a sliver of cantaloupe or avocado; sliced tomatoes and sweet onions flavored with mint, or any of hundreds of other combinations. Pita is also a good choice for sandwiches for small children because the pockets are easy to hold and eat.

For a supereasy picnic, carry pitas, sliced vegetables and meats, and yogurt dressing in separate containers and let your guests invent their own combinations. Take along a vacuum bottle of old-fashioned lemonade and serve cookies and slices of cold melon for dessert.

Although pita is widely available in supermarkets, we've provided an easy-to-make recipe, which you can bake ahead and freeze.

We have included many other sandwich-making hints in the recipes themselves. But we do have one final suggestion: take the time to read through the complete collection of cold sandwiches. There's a whole world of lunchtime treats collected here.

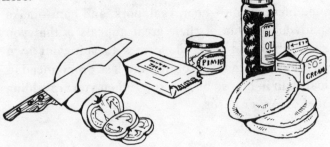

Roast Beef, Spinach, and Orange Rolls
MAKES 4 SANDWICHES

4 crusty sandwich rolls, split
Mayonnaise or Horseradish Mayonnaise
¾ to 1 pound roast beef, sliced thin
Salt and black pepper to taste
2 oranges, peeled and sliced
About ¼ pound spinach leaves
4 paper-thin slices sweet onion (optional)

Spread rolls thinly with mayonnaise, then arrange meat on bottoms. If necessary, season with salt and pepper. Top with orange slices and spinach. Add onion slices if desired. Cover with tops.

Note: You can substitute thinly sliced ham for the beef.

Roast Beef and Blue Cheese on Pumpernickel Bread
MAKES 2 SANDWICHES

4 slices pumpernickel
2 tablespoons mayonnaise
2 ounces blue cheese
About ½ pound roast beef, sliced thin
6 thin slices tomato
8 to 12 paper-thin slices cucumber
1 cup finely shredded Chinese cabbage

Spread 2 slices bread with mayonnaise and cover with thin slices blue cheese. Top with beef slices, tomatoes, cucumbers, Chinese cabbage, and remaining 2 slices of bread.

Roast Beef and Salad in Pita Pockets
MAKES 6 SANDWICHES

3½ cups shredded romaine lettuce
2 scallions, chopped
6 radishes, thinly sliced
¼ cup Italian salad dressing
3 large Pita loaves
6 tablespoons butter
¾ to 1 pound thinly sliced roast beef
Salt and black pepper to taste

Toss lettuce, scallions, and radishes with dressing. Cut pita loaves in half and spread insides with butter. Divide roast beef evenly among pockets, season with salt and pepper, and top with salad mixture.

Corned Beef and Coleslaw on Rye Bread
MAKES 2 SANDWICHES

Coleslaw (recipe below)
4 slices Sour Rye Bread
6 to 8 thin slices cooked corned beef
Prepared mustard

Spread coleslaw on 2 slices of bread. Top with corned beef. Spread remaining bread with a little mustard and close sandwiches.

Coleslaw

2 tablespoons mayonnaise
1 teaspoon drained prepared horseradish
1 teaspoon prepared mustard
1 teaspoon celery seed
1 cup shredded cabbage

Combine mayonnaise, horseradish, mustard, and celery seed, spoon over cabbage, and toss to mix thoroughly.

Minted Lamb on White Bread
MAKES 4 SANDWICHES

½ cup Blender Mayonnaise
2 teaspoons chopped fresh spearmint or dry spearmint
    soaked in small amount of warm water
1 scallion, chopped
Black pepper to taste
8 slices firm-textured white bread
8 or more slices cold roast lamb
4 Boston lettuce leaves

In a small bowl combine mayonnaise, mint, scallion, and pepper. Spread on 4 slices of bread. Top with slices of lamb, lettuce, and remaining 4 slices of bread.

Pork and Curried Coleslaw on a Bun
MAKES 4 SANDWICHES

2 tablespoons butter
4 Seeded Whole Wheat Sandwich Buns, split and toasted
8 slices roast pork loin, at room temperature
Curried Coleslaw (recipe below)

Lightly butter bottoms of buns and place 2 slices pork on each.
Add a layer of drained coleslaw and cover with tops.

Curried Coleslaw
¼ cup sour cream
¼ cup mayonnaise
½ to 1 teaspoon curry powder
1 teaspoon lemon juice
2 cups finely shredded green cabbage

Combine sour cream, mayonnaise, curry powder, and lemon
juice and stir to blend thoroughly. Combine dressing with
shredded cabbage and toss to blend.

Ham and Turkey Club
MAKES 4 SANDWICHES

The classic club is a three-decker sandwich (usually on white
toast) made with sliced turkey, crisp bacon, sliced tomato, lettuce, and mayonnaise. This one also includes ham, which
raises an already delectable combination to even greater
heights.

12 slices white bread, toasted
Mayonnaise
¼ pound sliced ham
8 slices crisp bacon
½ pound thinly sliced cooked turkey or chicken
8 paper-thin slices tomato
4 lettuce leaves
Small olives or pickles (optional)

Spread one side of each toast slice with mayonnaise. On 4 slices layer ham and bacon, cutting ham to fit. Cover each with a slice of toast, then top with turkey or chicken, tomato, lettuce, and the remaining toast. Push wooden picks into each sandwich about halfway between corners. Cut sandwiches diagonally in quarters. Serve with the picks, but be sure to point them out if they do not have decorated tops. Or plain toothpicks might be topped with small olives or pickles.

Ham and Cheese Heroes
MAKES 4 SANDWICHES

4 hero rolls or 1 long loaf Italian or French bread, split
    open halfway
About ½ cup mayonnaise
¼ head iceberg lettuce, finely shredded
½ pound boiled ham slices, halved
½ pound sliced mild cheese (Muenster, process American,
    Swiss)
2 tomatoes, sliced
1 large sweet onion, thinly sliced
Basil to taste
Oil and vinegar or hot pepper relish (optional)

Spread cut surfaces of roll generously with mayonnaise and fill with lettuce, ham, cheese, tomato, and onion. Sprinkle with basil. Use serrated or sharp knife to cut long-loaf hero in quarters. Serve with more mayonnaise, oil and vinegar, or hot pepper relish, if desired.

Ham and Asparagus Roll-Ups
MAKES 4 SANDWICHES

Mayonnaise
1 teaspoon lemon juice, or to taste
Few drops hot pepper sauce
4 large crisp-cooked asparagus spears
8 thin slices boiled ham
4 Boston lettuce leaves
4 frankfurter rolls

Combine ¼ cup mayonnaise, lemon juice, and pepper sauce and mix thoroughly. Place asparagus on 2 overlapping slices of ham, spread with seasoned mayonnaise, and roll up. Place a lettuce leaf on each roll with ham roll-up. You may spread the rolls with a teaspoon or so of mayonnaise if desired.

Ham and Apple Roll-Ups
MAKES 4 SANDWICHES

1 red-skinned eating apple, finely chopped
¼ cup finely chopped walnuts
⅓ cup mayonnaise
1 teaspoon lemon juice, or to taste
Ground ginger to taste
8 thin slices boiled ham
4 Boston lettuce leaves
4 frankfurter rolls

Combine apple, walnuts, mayonnaise, and lemon juice and season with a sprinkling of ginger. Spoon evenly on double ham slices and roll up to form tube. Place one lettuce leaf on each roll and top with ham roll-ups.

Ham Salad with Olives on White Bread
MAKES 6 SANDWICHES

1½ cups minced or ground cooked smoked ham
½ cup finely chopped celery
Mayonnaise
2 tablespoons minced green olives
1 tablespoon prepared mustard
1 tablespoon grated onion
Black pepper
12 slices White Wheat Germ Bread
4 to 6 leaves romaine lettuce, shredded

In a small bowl combine ham, celery, ⅓ cup mayonnaise, olives, mustard, and grated onion. Mix thoroughly and season to taste with pepper. Refrigerate to chill well. Spread ham salad on 6 slices of bread, top with lettuce, spread remaining 6 slices with mayonnaise, and close sandwiches.

Ham and Peanut Salad on Cornmeal Bread
MAKES 4 SANDWICHES

1½ cups diced cooked ham
¼ cup chopped salted peanuts
½ cup diced celery
1 tablespoon minced parsley
4 tablespoons Mustard Mayonnaise
8 slices Golden Cornmeal Yeast Bread or cracked wheat
    bread
4 lettuce leaves

In a bowl mix ham, peanuts, celery, parsley, and Mustard Mayonnaise. Stir to blend thoroughly. Spread mixture on 4 slices of bread. Top with lettuce and with remaining slices of bread.

Note: You may substitute ¼ cup toasted slivered blanched almonds for the peanuts.

Ham and Egg Salad Roll
MAKES 6 SANDWICHES

2 cups finely chopped cooked ham
½ cup diced celery
½ green pepper, minced
1 hard-cooked egg, chopped
6 tablespoons mayonnaise
½ teaspoon ground ginger
2 teaspoons lemon juice
1 tablespoon Dijon mustard
6 hard rolls
6 leaves Boston lettuce

In a bowl, mix together the ham, celery, green pepper, egg, mayonnaise, ginger, lemon juice, and mustard. Stir to blend thoroughly. Divide ham salad evenly and spread on bottoms of rolls. Top with lettuce, and then with tops of rolls.

Spicy Tongue and Zucchini Roll
MAKES 4 SANDWICHES

1 tablespoon malt or other vinegar
1 tablespoon prepared mustard
1 tablespoon water
About 1 cup sliced zucchini
4 sandwich rolls, split
About ¾ pound sliced cooked smoked tongue
Salt and black pepper to taste

Stir vinegar, mustard, and water together until smooth. Add zucchini and toss slices to coat. Cover and refrigerate 1 to 2 hours to blend flavors; drain. Arrange several zucchini slices on bottom of each roll. Sprinkle tongue lightly with salt and pepper and arrange on zucchini. Close sandwiches.

Egg Salad and Bologna on White Bread
MAKES 3 SANDWICHES

3 hard-cooked eggs
2 tablespoons mayonnaise
¼ teaspoon salt
Dash of black pepper
6 slices of white bread, toasted if desired
3 paper-thin slices onion (preferably sweet)
6 slices bologna
6 very thin slices tomato
3 lettuce leaves

Chop eggs coarsely and combine with mayonnaise, salt, and pepper. Spread on 3 bread slices; top with onion, bologna, tomato, lettuce, and remaining bread slices.

Meat Loaf and Beets on Whole Wheat Bread
MAKES 4 SANDWICHES

About ¼ cup mayonnaise
1 teaspoon drained prepared horseradish, or to taste
8 slices whole wheat bread, toasted if desired
8 thin slices cold meat loaf
About ¾ cup sliced pickled beets or sweet pickles
4 lettuce leaves
Salt and black pepper to taste

Combine mayonnaise and horseradish and spread on bread slices. Arrange meat loaf on 4 slices; top with beets or pickles and lettuce. Sprinkle with salt and pepper and top with remaining bread.

Olive Meat Loaf
MAKES ENOUGH FOR 6 TO 8 SANDWICHES

A hearty loaf that makes delicious sandwiches—either hot or cold. You can also make it with veal. Season the veal loaf with crushed rosemary instead of oregano.

1½ pounds ground beef
½ cup bread crumbs
1 egg
1 small onion, grated or very finely minced
1 teaspoon salt
¼ teaspoon black pepper
½ teaspoon oregano
1 tablespoon finely chopped parsley
¾ cup salad olives (chopped green olives and pimientos)

Combine all ingredients except olives and mix thoroughly. Add olives and stir or knead to distribute evenly. Shape into a loaf and place on a lightly greased pan. Bake in a 350° F. oven for 1 hour. Allow to cool before slicing.

Old-Fashioned Veal Loaf on Crusty Italian Bread
MAKES 12 SANDWICHES

This richly seasoned, peppery loaf makes wonderful sandwiches, especially when served on crusty Italian or French bread. It's also great on Challah or Savory Cottage Cheese Bread. If veal is not available (check with your butcher if you don't see it), then this is almost as good when made with ground round.

    2 pounds ground veal
    1 cup soft bread crumbs
    1 clove garlic, crushed or pressed
    ¼ cup grated onion
    ½ cup chopped parsley
    2 tablespoons lemon juice
    2 eggs, lightly beaten
    1 teaspoon thyme
    1 teaspoon salt
    1 tablespoon cracked black pepper
    ¼ cup butter or margarine melted with ¼ cup water
    12 rolls Crusty Italian Bread
    6 tablespoons butter or margarine
    12 leaves romaine lettuce, shredded
    Prepared mustard (optional)

In a large bowl combine veal, bread crumbs, garlic, onion, parsley, lemon juice, eggs, thyme, salt, and pepper. Blend thoroughly with hands or a mixing spoon. Shape into a loaf and place in a shallow baking pan. Bake in a preheated 350° F. oven for 1 hour, basting occasionally with butter and water combination. Cool before slicing.

Split Italian rolls and lightly spread bottoms with butter or margarine. Put 2 slices veal loaf on each, top with shredded romaine, spread tops of rolls with mustard if desired, and close loaves.

Savory Pork Loaf on Rye Bread
MAKES 6 SANDWICHES

1 pound lean ground pork
1 cup soft bread crumbs
1 egg, slightly beaten
¼ cup milk, or skim milk if desired
2 tablespoons grated onion
½ teaspoon poultry seasoning
1 teaspoon salt
¼ teaspoon black pepper, or more to taste
12 slices Sour Rye Bread or other rye bread
Butter
6 Boston lettuce leaves
Prepared mustard

In a medium bowl combine pork, bread crumbs, egg, milk, onion, and seasonings and mix to blend thoroughly. Shape into loaf, place in a shallow baking pan, and bake in 350° F. preheated oven for about 1 hour. Cool before slicing.

Spread 6 slices bread lightly with butter, top with 2 slices pork loaf, add lettuce leaves, spread remaining bread slices with mustard, and close sandwiches.

Ham and Veal Loaf on Whole Wheat Sandwich Buns

MAKES 12 SANDWICHES

A zesty ham loaf that is scented with cloves and enlivened by the addition of horseradish. These buns are ideal to serve when friends drop over to watch the game on a Sunday afternoon. They're delicious with cold beer or hot cider.

1½ pounds ground cooked ham
½ pound ground veal or pork
2 eggs
1½ cups fine dry bread crumbs
1 teaspoon prepared mustard
1 tablespoon prepared horseradish
2 tablespoons grated onion
¼ teaspoon salt
¼ teaspoon black pepper
¾ cup milk
8 to 10 whole cloves
½ cup orange juice
12 Seeded Whole Wheat Sandwich Buns
6 tablespoons butter or margarine
Spicy brown mustard (optional)

In a large mixing bowl combine ham, veal or pork, eggs, bread crumbs, mustard, horseradish, onion, seasonings, and milk. Mix with hands or with a large spoon to blend all ingredients thoroughly. Shape into a loaf and put in a shallow baking pan. Score top with diamond shapes with back of knife and stud loaf with cloves. Bake in a 350° F. oven for 1½ hours, basting occasionally with orange juice mixed with an equal amount of water. Cool before slicing.

Split sandwich buns, butter bottom halves, and put 2 slices ham loaf on each. Spread top halves with mustard if desired and close sandwiches.

Braunschweiger and Carrot Rolls
MAKES 4 SANDWICHES

⅔ cup shredded carrot
3 tablespoons Horseradish Mayonnaise
Dash of pepper
4 sandwich rolls, split
½ pound thinly sliced braunschweiger or liverwurst
8 slices crisp bacon

Combine carrot, Horseradish Mayonnaise, and pepper. If desired, spread roll bottoms with a little additional mayonnaise. Put braunschweiger or liverwurst slices on roll bottoms; top with carrot mixture, then with bacon slices. Cover with roll tops and serve at once.

Liverwurst Plus

Good liverwurst is an old favorite that is sometimes overlooked. Try one of these special combinations for a satisfying taste experience.

- ► Liverwurst, sliced sweet red onion on Sour Rye Bread or pumpernickel
- ► Liverwurst, chopped green onion, Swiss cheese on whole wheat bread
- ► Liverwurst, sliced raw mushrooms, watercress, spicy brown mustard on Finnish-Style Health Bread
- ► Liverwurst, green pepper slices, Boston lettuce on Seeded Whole Wheat Sandwich Buns

Dried Beef and Cheese Spread on Rye Bread
MAKES 6 SANDWICHES

2 cups (about ½ pound) shredded Cheddar cheese
3 ounces cream cheese, softened
¼ cup minced green pepper
1 tablespoon grated onion
1 small clove garlic, minced
2½-ounce jar dried beef, chopped fine
Freshly ground black pepper to taste
About ⅓ cup milk
12 slices Sour Rye Bread

In small bowl of mixer mix cheeses, green pepper, onion, garlic, beef, and pepper. Beat in enough milk for creamy spreading consistency. Cover and chill several hours or overnight to blend flavors. Remove from refrigerator about 30 minutes before serving. Spread on 6 slices of bread and cover with remaining slices.

Note: This spread is also delicious served on crackers or small slices of assorted breads as a canapé.

Sliced Chicken and Watercress on White Bread
MAKES 2 SANDWICHES

4 slices White Wheat Germ Bread
Tarragon- or basil-flavored mayonnaise
1 chicken breast, cooked and sliced
6 to 8 sprigs of watercress, coarse stems removed
Salt and black pepper

Spread bread slices lightly with mayonnaise. Cover 2 slices with sliced chicken and watercress sprigs. Sprinkle with salt and pepper to taste. Cover with remaining bread.

Oriental Sliced Chicken and Bean Sprouts on Sesame Whole Wheat Bread
MAKES 3 SANDWICHES

About ¾ cup fresh or drained canned bean sprouts
1 tablespoon sliced scallions
2 tablespoons chopped radishes
1 teaspoon soy sauce
6 slices Sesame Whole Wheat Bread
2 tablespoons mayonnaise
About 1½ chicken breasts, cooked and sliced thin
Salt to taste
3 lettuce leaves

Combine sprouts, scallions, radishes, and soy sauce. Let stand 30 minutes to blend flavors, then drain well. Spread bread slices with mayonnaise. Arrange chicken on 3 slices and sprinkle with salt. Top with lettuce and sprout mixture. Close sandwiches.

Sliced Chicken, Avocado, and Spinach on Challah
MAKES 2 SANDWICHES

4 slices Challah
2 to 3 tablespoons Curried Mayonnaise
1 small avocado, peeled and sliced
1 chicken breast, cooked and sliced
8 to 12 spinach leaves, washed, with coarse stems removed

Spread bread lightly with mayonnaise, cover 2 slices with avocado, chicken, and spinach, and top with remaining bread.

Chicken Salad with Almonds on a Roll
MAKES 6 SANDWICHES

3 cups diced cooked chicken
½ cup golden raisins
½ cup toasted slivered blanched almonds
3 ribs celery, diced
¾ cup mayonnaise
¼ cup orange juice
6 crusty sandwich rolls
1 bunch watercress, coarse stems removed

In a bowl combine chicken, raisins, almonds, celery, mayonnaise, and orange juice. Toss to blend thoroughly. Spread chicken salad on roll halves, top with 4 or 5 sprigs of watercress, and cover with roll tops.

Chicken Salad with Grapes on Whole Wheat Bread
MAKES 4 SANDWICHES

2 cups diced cooked chicken
2 green onions, chopped
½ cup diced celery
½ cup seedless grapes, cut in half
¼ cup mayonnaise
¼ cup sour cream
Salt and black pepper to taste
8 slices whole wheat bread
4 leaves romaine lettuce

In a small bowl combine chicken, onions, celery, and grapes. Combine mayonnaise and sour cream and add to chicken mixture. Toss to blend thoroughly and taste for seasoning. Add salt and pepper if necessary. Spread chicken salad on 4 slices of bread, cover with romaine, and top with remaining bread slices.

Other Chicken Salad Sandwiches

- ▸ Diced chicken, chopped unpeeled red apple, chives, Curried Mayonnaise on White Wheat Germ Bread
- ▸ Diced chicken, chopped green pepper, Russian Dressing on Sour Rye Bread
- ▸ Diced chicken, chopped scallions, chopped black olives, mayonnaise on Crusty Italian Bread

Chopped Chicken Liver on Rye Bread
MAKES 3 SANDWICHES

This is an authentic Jewish recipe for a much-loved favorite.

2 to 3 tablespoons chicken fat or butter
1 medium onion, finely chopped
½ pound chicken livers
2 hard-cooked eggs
Salt and freshly ground black pepper
6 slices rye bread
Garlic pickles

Heat 2 tablespoons chicken fat or butter in a frying pan and sauté the onions until soft and golden. Add the chicken livers (and 1 or 2 teaspoons of chicken fat if necessary) and cook over medium heat for about 5 minutes, until livers are lightly brown and cooked through. Combine the livers, onions, and eggs in a chopping bowl and chop fine. (You may also use a food processor for this step.) Add salt and pepper to taste and remaining chicken fat if necessary. The mixture should be smooth and moist but not too soft. Spread thickly on 3 slices of bread and top with remaining bread. Serve with garlic pickles.

Chicken Liver Pâté on a Muffin
MAKES 4 SANDWICHES

A variation on the classic recipe for chicken liver spread, this is also delightful.

½ pound chicken livers
3 tablespoons chopped onion
2 tablespoons butter or margarine
¼ cup minced celery
1 hard-cooked egg, chopped
1 tablespoon chopped olives
Mayonnaise
Salt and black pepper to taste
4 English muffins, bagels, or bialys, split and toasted
4 paper-thin slices red onion (optional)
4 lettuce leaves

Sauté livers and onion in hot butter or margarine until livers are of desired doneness. Cool slightly, then chop. Add celery, egg, olives, and 1 tablespoon mayonnaise. Season with salt and pepper. Spread bread with mayonnaise. Spread half the bread with liver mixture, then top with onion slices, lettuce, and remaining bread halves.

Curried Egg Salad on Sourdough Bread
MAKES 4 SANDWICHES

6 hard-cooked eggs, chopped
4 to 6 tablespoons mayonnaise
1 teaspoon curry powder
½ cup stuffed olives, chopped
¼ teaspoon salt, or more to taste
¼ teaspoon black pepper
8 slices white sourdough bread
4 leaves romaine lettuce, shredded

In a small bowl combine eggs, mayonnaise (using only enough to moisten well), curry powder, olives, salt, and pepper. Stir to blend well. Spread egg mixture on 4 slices of bread, top with lettuce, and cover with remaining bread slices.

Egg Salad Plus

Fresh-tasting chopped egg combined with homemade mayonnaise is one of the most popular of all sandwich fillings. And when you add flavor highlights, such as chopped fresh basil, capers and grated lemon rind, chopped watercress, or sliced red radishes, you can create a whole array of delightful variations on the theme. Here are some of our favorites.

Add just enough mayonnaise to chopped hard-cooked egg to moisten well. Then add any of these flavorings and garnishes:

- ▸ Capers, grated lemon rind on Buttermilk Cheese Bread
- ▸ Chopped scallions, chopped radish, raw spinach leaves on Finnish-Style Health Bread
- ▸ Chopped celery, chopped chives, watercress sprigs on Seeded Whole Wheat Sandwich Buns

► Chopped pimiento olives, sliced cucumber, romaine lettuce on Sour Rye Bread

► Chopped fresh dill or dried dillweed, sunflower seeds, sliced tomato on White Wheat Germ Bread

► Chopped boiled ham, minced sweet onion, chopped green pepper on Golden Cornmeal Yeast Bread

► Chopped dill pickle, sliced green pepper on Honey Oatmeal Bread

Bayou Crab in Pita Pockets
MAKES 3 SANDWICHES

½ cup chopped celery
¼ cup chopped onion
¼ cup parsley sprigs (not packed)
2 tablespoons vinegar
1 tablespoon prepared mustard
½ teaspoon prepared horseradish
1 teaspoon paprika
¼ teaspoon black pepper
⅛ teaspoon hot pepper sauce
½ cup mayonnaise
6 or 8 ounces crab meat, thawed if frozen, drained, and flaked fine
1 cup shredded lettuce
3 loaves Pita, halved and opened, or 6 slices white bread, toasted

In blender container combine celery, onion, parsley, vinegar, mustard, horseradish, paprika, pepper, and pepper sauce and whirl until smooth. Stir into mayonnaise. Combine about half the mayonnaise mixture with crab and lettuce and spoon into pita pockets. Pass remaining sauce to spoon over crab filling. If toast is used, add all the mayonnaise mixture to crab and fill 3 closed sandwiches.

Shrimp Salad and Avocado on Savory Cottage Cheese Bread

MAKES 4 SANDWICHES

1 cup chopped cooked shrimps
2 teaspoons chopped scallions
2 tablespoons chopped celery
¼ cup mayonnaise
1 teaspoon lemon juice
Dash of hot pepper sauce
½ teaspoon sweet paprika
8 slices Savory Cottage Cheese Bread or other firm-
    textured white bread
8 slices ripe avocado
3 or 4 romaine leaves, shredded

In a bowl combine chopped shrimps, scallions, celery, mayonnaise, lemon juice, pepper sauce, and paprika. Stir to mix
thoroughly. Spread shrimp salad in four equal portions on 4
slices of bread; top with avocado, shredded lettuce, and remaining slices of bread.

Note: For a curried shrimp salad, use Curried Mayonnaise instead of plain.

Shrimp Salad in Pita Pockets
MAKES 4 SANDWICHES

2 cups cooked shrimps, coarsely chopped
½ cup sliced celery
¼ cup diced green pepper
2 tablespoons mayonnaise
1 tablespoon catsup or chili sauce
1 tablespoon chopped onion
1½ teaspoons diced pimiento (optional)
1½ teaspoons capers (optional)
Salt and black pepper to taste
4 loaves Pita, halved
Romaine lettuce leaves

Combine shrimps, celery, green pepper, mayonnaise, catsup or chili sauce, onion, and optional pimiento and capers. Chill well. Season with salt and pepper. Open pockets of pita, line with romaine, and spoon in shrimp mixture.

Salmon Salad and Cucumber Roll
MAKES 4 SANDWICHES

16-ounce can salmon, chilled
¼ cup chopped celery
½ cup mayonnaise
2 tablespoons minced scallions
1 tablespoon minced parsley
¼ teaspoon tarragon
¼ teaspoon salt
Dash of black pepper
4 crusty sandwich rolls, split
Marinated Cucumber Slices, drained (recipe below)
4 lettuce leaves

Drain salmon well, discard any bones, then flake fish coarsely. Stir in celery and set aside. Combine mayonnaise, scallions, parsley, tarragon, salt, and pepper. Spread about 3 tablespoons on rolls. Stir remaining mayonnaise mixture into salmon. Spoon generously on roll bottoms. Top with some cucumber slices, lettuce leaf, and roll tops.

Marinated Cucumber Slices
In small bowl combine ½ medium cucumber, sliced thin, ¼ cup white vinegar, 2 teaspoons sugar, and ¼ teaspoon salt. Cover and refrigerate 1 to 2 hours.

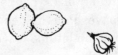

Salmon with Cream Cheese on Pumpernickel Bread
MAKES 3 SANDWICHES

3 ounces cream cheese, at room temperature
3½-ounce can salmon, well drained
1 teaspoon lemon juice
½ teaspoon prepared mustard
¼ teaspoon seasoned salt
Dash of hot pepper sauce
¼ teaspoon paprika
2 teaspoons finely chopped scallions
6 slices dark pumpernickel bread
12 sprigs of watercress

In a medium bowl combine cream cheese, salmon, lemon juice, mustard, seasoned salt, hot pepper sauce, and paprika and stir to blend thoroughly. Sprinkle in scallions and stir again. Spread on 3 slices of pumpernickel, cover with 4 watercress sprigs, and top with remaining slices of bread.

Fish Salad Rolls
MAKES 4 SANDWICHES

2 cups coarsely flaked Poached Fish (recipe below)
¼ cup chopped parsley
Mayonnaise
2 tablespoons sliced scallions, including tops
1 teaspoon lemon juice
Salt and black pepper to taste
4 sandwich rolls, split
4 lettuce leaves

Mix lightly fish, parsley, ¼ cup mayonnaise, scallions, and lemon juice. Add salt and pepper. Spread roll bottoms with mayonnaise if desired, then top each with a generous spoonful of fish mixture and a lettuce leaf; close rolls.

Poached Fish
In large skillet bring 2 cups water to boil; add 1 teaspoon salt and ¼ teaspoon black pepper or peppercorns. (For special flavor add 1 sliced small onion, ½ teaspoon tarragon, a little parsley, and a lemon slice.) Simmer 10 minutes, then add about 1 pound fish fillets and simmer 5 minutes longer or until fish flakes easily with fork. Drain well; cool completely.

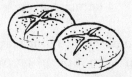

Egg and Sardine Spread on Whole Wheat Bread
MAKES 4 SANDWICHES

3 hard-cooked eggs
4⅜-ounce can skinless boneless sardines, drained
.4 tablespoons butter or margarine, softened
¼ cup finely chopped scallions with tops
1 tablespoon prepared mustard
1 tablespoon lemon juice
½ teaspoon salt, or to taste
Dash of hot pepper sauce
8 slices Sesame Whole Wheat Bread

With fork, mash eggs and sardines to a paste in large bowl. Add remaining ingredients (except bread) and mix well. Spread on 4 slices bread and top with remaining slices.

Sardines with Herb Butter on a Roll
MAKES 4 SANDWICHES

¼ cup butter or margarine, softened
1 tablespoon chopped parsley
1½ teaspoons freeze-dried chives
1 teaspoon lemon juice
¼ teaspoon tarragon
4 soft sandwich rolls or English muffins, split and toasted
Two 3¾-ounce cans sardines, drained
4 lettuce leaves

Combine butter or margarine, parsley, chives, lemon juice, and tarragon. Spread on rolls or muffins. Arrange sardines on roll or muffin bottoms and top with lettuce and roll or muffin tops.

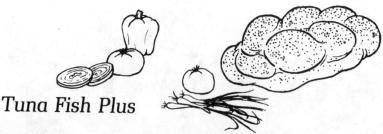

Tuna Fish Plus

Americans love tuna more than almost any other sandwich filling. In fact, we have heard of people who like it so much they have a tuna salad sandwich for lunch every single working day. Much as we ourselves like this tasty gift from the sea, we find the idea of daily tuna sandwiches is overdoing a good thing. But we do know some wonderful ways to vary tuna, including an appealing salade niçoise in pita, as well as a super curried tuna salad with crisp chunks of apple. So even if you think you've found the perfect recipe for tuna salad, we hope you'll try some of the delectable combinations offered below.

Start with basic tuna salad: Use approximately 2 tablespoons mayonnaise and about ½ to 1 teaspoon lemon juice for each 3½-ounce can of tuna. Then combine with any of the following:

- Chopped scallion, chopped parsley, very thin slices of peeled lemon on White Wheat Germ Bread
- Capers, scallions, grated lemon rind on Buttermilk Cheese Bread
- Chopped chives, chopped parsley, thinly sliced cucumber, Boston lettuce on Sesame Whole Wheat Bread
- Chopped celery, chopped scallions, tomato slices on Challah
- Chopped green pepper, watercress, sliced radishes on Finnish-Style Health Bread
- Chopped cucumber, halved cherry tomatoes, romaine lettuce on Seeded Whole Wheat Sandwich Buns
- Chopped parsley, lemon juice, sliced red onion on Sour Rye Bread

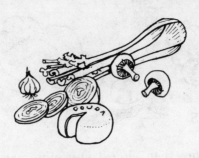

Tuna Salade Niçoise in Pita Pocket

MAKES 4 SANDWICHES

7-ounce can tuna fish, drained and flaked
¼ cup Vinaigrette Dressing (recipe below)
4 large leaves romaine lettuce
4 loaves Pita, sliced across the top
2 medium tomatoes, halved and sliced
4 hard-cooked eggs, sliced
16 green beans, blanched and chilled
Salt and black pepper to taste

In a small bowl combine tuna fish and vinaigrette and toss to mix thoroughly. Shred lettuce leaves and place one in each pita, top with sliced tomatoes, sliced eggs, green beans, and then with tuna. Sprinkle with salt and pepper. Moisten with additional vinaigrette, if desired.

Vinaigrette Dressing

MAKES ½ CUP

3 tablespoons white wine or red wine vinegar
9 tablespoons safflower oil
½ clove garlic, crushed
Salt and freshly ground black pepper to taste

Combine all ingredients in a small bowl and stir to blend thoroughly.

Curried Tuna Salad with Apple on Sesame Whole Wheat Bread
MAKES 4 SANDWICHES

7-ounce can tuna fish flaked
½ cup diced celery
¼ cup chopped toasted almonds
½ cup chopped red apple, unpeeled
½ cup mayonnaise
2 teaspoons lemon juice
½ teaspoon curry powder
8 slices Sesame Whole Wheat Bread

Mix flaked tuna, celery, almonds, apple, mayonnaise, lemon juice, and curry powder and stir to blend thoroughly. Spread on 4 slices bread and top with remaining slices.

Pineapple-Tuna Salad Rolls
MAKES 4 SANDWICHES

6½- or 7-ounce can tuna, undrained
½ cup finely diced celery
½ cup crushed pineapple, drained well
2 tablespoons diced green pepper
½ teaspoon ground ginger
¼ teaspoon salt, or to taste
Dash of black pepper
4 sandwich rolls, toasted if desired and cooled
4 lettuce leaves

Flake tuna coarsely; add celery, pineapple, green pepper, ginger, salt, and pepper. Spoon into sandwich rolls, top with lettuce, and close rolls. Serve at once.

Cheese Sandwiches

There are so many delicious American and imported cheeses that there are whole books devoted to the subject. If you find yourself confined to just a few of these—Cheddar, Swiss, and Muenster—start experimenting now. Here are just a few of our favorite cheese combinations:

- ▸ Brie, sliced pear, watercress on Finnish-Style Health Bread
- ▸ Mozzarella, sliced tomato, fresh basil on Italian bread
- ▸ Gorgonzola, spinach, sliced red onion, mayonnaise on Seeded Whole Wheat Sandwich Buns
- ▸ Monterey Jack, sliced avocado, sprouts, sliced tomato on Sesame Whole Wheat Bread

Cream Cheese, Blue Cheese, and Watercress on Whole Wheat Bread
MAKES 2 SANDWICHES

Butter or margarine
4 slices whole wheat or rye bread
3 ounces cream cheese
⅛ pound blue cheese
1 tablespoon skim milk
2 tablespoons chopped toasted almonds
10 to 12 sprigs watercress

Lightly butter the bread. In a small bowl soften cream cheese with a fork; add blue cheese and mash with the fork. Stir to blend thoroughly. Add milk and almonds and stir to blend. Spread half the cheese mixture on each of 2 slices of bread. Lay watercress on cheese and top with remaining slices of bread.

Blue Cheese and Bacon on White Toast
MAKES 3 SANDWICHES

6 slices white bread, toasted
Mayonnaise
About 3 ounces blue or Roquefort cheese, sliced thin or
  crumbled
6 or 9 slices crisp bacon
Lettuce leaves

Spread toast with mayonnaise, then arrange cheese on 3 slices.
Top with bacon, lettuce, and remaining toast slices.

Herbed Feta Cheese in Pita Pockets
MAKES 4 SANDWICHES

¾ pound feta cheese
1 cup olive oil, or half olive oil and half safflower oil
¼ cup lemon juice
2 tablespoons minced scallions, including some of the
  green tops
1 medium clove garlic, minced (optional)
½ teaspoon oregano
½ teaspoon salt
Dash of hot pepper sauce
4 loaves Pita, warmed in oven and sliced across top
2 medium tomatoes, chopped
1 small head romaine lettuce, shredded

Cut feta into ¾-inch cubes (you will have 2½ cups of cubes) and
place in ceramic bowl. Combine oil, lemon juice, scallions, garlic, oregano, salt, and pepper sauce, and pour over cheese.
Cover bowl with plastic wrap and marinate for at least 2 hours.

Drain cheese and place 4 cubes in each pita half. Add tomatoes, lettuce, and 1 tablespoon marinade to each sandwich.

Cream Cheese, Carrots, and Raisins on Cracked Wheat Bread
MAKES 4 SANDWICHES

Two 3-ounce packages cream cheese, softened
½ cup raisins
1 tablespoon grated lemon rind
2 teaspoons lemon juice
1 carrot, grated
2 tablespoons toasted sesame seeds
8 slices cracked wheat bread

In a small bowl combine cream cheese, raisins, lemon rind, lemon juice, carrot, and sesame seeds. Stir to blend thoroughly. Spread cheese mixture on 4 slices of bread and top with remaining slices of bread.

Cottage Cheese, Chicken, and Pineapple on Whole Wheat Bread
MAKES 4 SANDWICHES

¾ cup creamed cottage cheese
½ teaspoon poppy seeds (optional)
¼ teaspoon salt
8 slices whole wheat bread, toasted if desired
4 canned pineapple slices, drained
4 thin slices smoked chicken, turkey, or ham

Combine cottage cheese, poppy seeds, and salt. Spread on 4 bread slices. Top with pineapple, meat, and remaining bread.

Cottage Cheese Plus

High in protein, low in calories, and creamy rich in texture, cottage cheese is a diet watcher's delight. And since this fresh-tasting cheese blends well with both sweet fruits and savory vegetables, it is one of the most versatile of all sandwich fillings. We recommend small-curd or whipped cottage cheese for sandwiches—either low-fat or regular. Here are some of our favorite cottage cheese combinations:

- ▶ Chopped dried apricots, toasted walnuts, watercress on Whole Wheat Walnut Raisin Bread
- ▶ Crushed pineapple, toasted almonds, butter, lettuce on Buttermilk Raisin Bread
- ▶ Chopped celery, scallions, grated carrot, cumin on Finnish-Style Health Bread
- ▶ Chopped radishes, sliced cucumber, romaine lettuce on White Wheat Germ Bread
- ▶ Chopped dates, orange rind, orange juice, sunflower seeds on Golden Cornmeal Yeast Bread
- ▶ Chopped watercress, scallions, chopped radishes on Sour Rye Bread
- ▶ Chopped green pepper, chopped celery, parsley on Sesame Whole Wheat Bread
- ▶ Chopped cucumber, celery seed, radishes, sprouts on Honey Oatmeal Bread

Avocado Sandwiches

Buttery rich avocado is a major ingredient in some of the most delicious vegetarian sandwiches. You can simply peel and slice it (add a sprinkling of lemon juice to prevent darkening) or you can mash and blend it into guacamole. It's great with green pepper, carrot, and sunflower seeds on whole wheat bread, or with fresh basil, Muenster, and sliced tomato, or with spinach, sliced egg, and mushroom.

Guacamole, Bacon, and Tomato on a Muffin
MAKES 3 SANDWICHES

½ medium avocado, peeled and mashed (about ½ cup)
1½ teaspoons lime juice, or to taste
1 teaspoon grated onion or 3 paper-thin slices onion
⅛ teaspoon salt
⅛ teaspoon hot pepper sauce
3 English muffins, split and toasted
9 slices crisp bacon
3 slices tomato
3 lettuce leaves

Combine avocado, lime juice, grated onion (if using it), salt, and pepper sauce. Spread on 3 muffin halves. Top each with 3 bacon slices, a tomato slice, an onion slice (if using instead of grated onion), a lettuce leaf, and remaining muffin half.

Avocado and Alfalfa Sprouts on Pumpernickel Bread
MAKES 3 SANDWICHES

1 medium avocado, peeled and sliced thin
Lemon juice
¼ cup butter or margarine, softened
1½ teaspoons prepared mustard
6 slices dark pumpernickel bread
Salt and pepper to taste
¾ cup alfalfa or bean sprouts
3 lettuce leaves

Sprinkle avocado slices with lemon juice to prevent darkening. Combine butter or margarine and mustard and spread on bread. Arrange avocado slices on 3 bread slices. Sprinkle with salt and pepper. Top each with ¼ cup sprouts, a lettuce leaf, and remaining bread slices.

Peanut Butter Plus

Some devoted peanut butter lovers—both children and adults—claim that the only way to fully savor the rich goodness of this delicacy is to eat it by the spoonful straight from the jar. We happen to like peanut butter best when it is spread on especially good bread (try our Buttermilk Raisin Bread, Golden Cornmeal Yeast Bread, or Seeded Whole Wheat Sandwich Buns) and combined with any one of a number of different fruits, vegetables, meats, or jams. Everybody we know seems to have one combination he loves best. There are people whose eyes glisten when they describe the delight of such medleys as peanut butter, pineapple, and spinach leaves or peanut butter, banana slices, and ham on Sesame Whole Wheat Bread. The possibilities are boundless. Here are just a few of our old favorites, peanut butter plus:

- ► Chopped dates, toasted sesame seeds, orange juice to moisten on Finnish-Style Health Bread
- ► Grated apple, lemon juice to moisten, apple butter, romaine lettuce on Challah
- ► Honey, chopped candied ginger, alfalfa sprouts on Sesame Whole Wheat Bread
- ► Grated carrot, raisins, milk to moisten on Golden Cornmeal Yeast Bread
- ► Crushed pineapple, sunflower seeds, pineapple juice to moisten on Buttermilk Raisin Bread
- ► Honey, banana slices, chopped walnuts, shredded romaine lettuce on Pita

▶ Orange marmalade, sunflower seeds, spinach leaves, orange juice to moisten on Sour Rye Bread
▶ Chutney, romaine lettuce, lemon juice to moisten on Seeded Whole Wheat Sandwich Buns

Bacon and Chunky Peanut Butter on Whole Wheat Walnut Raisin Toast
MAKES 8 SANDWICHES

1 cup chunky-style peanut butter
3 tablespoons mayonnaise
2 teaspoons lemon juice
1 cup finely diced, pared Golden Delicious apple
16 slices Whole Wheat Walnut Raisin bread
16 slices crisp bacon
8 leaves Boston lettuce

Combine peanut butter, mayonnaise, and lemon juice and stir to blend thoroughly. Stir in apple. Toast bread. Spread 8 pieces of toast with peanut butter–apple mixture; top each with 2 slices of bacon and 1 lettuce leaf. Cover with remaining slices of toast.

Peanut Butter, Ham, and Banana on Whole Wheat Bread
MAKES 4 SANDWICHES

8 slices whole wheat bread
Softened butter or margarine (optional)
¼ to ½ cup chunky-style peanut butter
2 small bananas, sliced
4 to 8 thin slices boiled ham

Spread bread slices with butter or margarine if desired, then spread 4 slices with 1 to 2 tablespoons each peanut butter. Arrange banana slices on peanut butter and top with ham and remaining bread.

Peanut Butter, Pear, and Watercress on Raisin Bread
MAKES 4 SANDWICHES

⅓ cup peanut butter
2 to 3 tablespoons honey
8 slices Buttermilk Raisin Bread or other raisin bread
1 medium pear, cored and sliced
16 sprigs of watercress

Combine peanut butter and honey. Spread on half the bread slices. Arrange pear slices on peanut butter; top with 4 watercress sprigs and remaining bread.

3 · THE PERFECT HAMBURGER AND OTHER HOT SANDWICH DELIGHTS

NOBODY HAS TO TAKE A POLL TO DISCOVER THAT AMERICANS ARE crazy about hamburgers. All across the country many fast-food restaurants and sandwich shops base their entire menu on this all-time favorite. Yet even though we may all agree that the hamburger is one of our top choices, there's still quite a bit of controversy over exactly how to prepare and cook the perfect hamburger—as well as lively debates over just what to use to garnish it for ultimate perfection. We hope to end more than a few arguments over the best cooking techniques by offering an unusually effective method we've kitchen-tested time and again with splendid results. On the other hand, we may be guilty of inciting brand-new disputes over garnishes with our collection of delectable toppings.

While hamburgers may be an odds-on favorite, there are any number of other hot sandwiches that get our vote. Naturally, we have included several first-rate hot dog recipes. And we offer savory pot roast; a mushroom, turkey, and mozzarella

72

combination; a ham soufflé sandwich; best-ever grilled cheese creations; barbecued turkey; grilled Canadian bacon, lettuce, and tomato; and old-fashioned fried bologna (you didn't think we'd forget that!). Some of these hot sandwiches are just right for festive brunches, others call to mind elegant suppers, and some are perfect any time. For the easiest entertaining ever, just serve one of these delicious sandwiches, a fresh-tasting green salad, fruit or another light dessert, and a special bottle of wine.

The Perfect Hamburger

To make the best, juiciest hamburgers, choose coarsely ground meat with 30 percent fat (called ground chuck or beef). Too-lean meat as well as vigorous handling and packing produce dry hamburgers.

Break off the amount of meat desired and shape very lightly into a patty. Use 5 ounces meat for the average serving; if topping is rich in protein, however (cheese, yogurt, sunflower seeds), use only 4 ounces meat.

To pan-broil hamburgers: Lightly brush heavy skillet with oil or sprinkle generously with salt; heat over moderately high heat 1 minute. Add hamburgers; cook, turning once, according to time below for desired doneness (do not press during cooking).

To broil: Place hamburgers on lightly greased rack. Broil in preheated broiler 3 inches from heat source, turning once, according to cooking time below.

Cooking time per side: For 5-ounce hamburger—5 to 6 minutes for rare, 7 minutes for medium, 8 to 9 minutes for well done. Decrease time 1 minute for 4-ounce hamburger.

Super Toppings for the Perfect Hamburger

Onion-Pepper Topping
MAKES ENOUGH TO TOP 4 HAMBURGERS
1 large onion, sliced
1 large green pepper, cut in ½-inch strips
2 tablespoons oil, preferably olive

In medium skillet sauté onion and green pepper in oil, stirring, until crisp-tender.

Health-Salad Topping
MAKES ENOUGH TO TOP 4 HAMBURGERS
1 cup shredded carrots
2 tablespoons plain yogurt
1 tablespoon plus 1 teaspoon wheat germ
½ teaspoon honey
2 teaspoons sunflower seeds

Mix well carrot, yogurt, 1 tablespoon wheat germ, and the honey; top 4 cooked hamburgers. Sprinkle with remaining 1 teaspoon wheat germ and the sunflower seeds.

Note: If desired, garnish with carrot curls.

North Sea Topping
MAKES ENOUGH TO TOP 1 HAMBURGER
1 tablespoon sour cream
½ teaspoon red caviar
½ teaspoon thinly sliced scallion

Layer sour cream and caviar on cooked hamburger; garnish with scallion.

Guacamole Topping
MAKES ENOUGH TO TOP 6 HAMBURGERS
1 medium avocado, mashed (1½ cups)
1 small tomato, seeded and chopped fine (⅓ cup)
Juice of ½ lemon (about 1 tablespoon)
1 clove garlic, crushed
½ teaspoon chili powder, or to taste
½ teaspoon salt
Dash of black pepper

Mix well all ingredients.

Note: If desired, place hamburger on top of fried tortilla, top with guacamole, and garnish with tomato and lemon wedges.

Cucumber Topping
MAKES ENOUGH TO TOP 6 HAMBURGERS
1 medium cucumber, peeled, seeded, and diced
½ teaspoon salt
2 tablespoons cottage cheese (see note)
1 tablespoon cider vinegar
1 teaspoon sugar
¼ teaspoon caraway seeds

Mix well cucumber and salt; let stand 10 minutes. Drain well. Stir in remaining ingredients. If desired, garnish with cucumber.

Note: Yogurt can be substituted for cottage cheese. Topping may get watery on standing; drain if necessary.

Artichoke-Pimiento Topping
MAKES ENOUGH TO TOP 1 HAMBURGER
1 tablespoon Green Mayonnaise (or green goddess dressing)
1 canned or fresh-cooked artichoke heart
½ large pimiento, cut in 3 leaf shapes

Pour dressing on cooked hamburger; place artichoke heart in center; arrange pimiento around artichoke.

Blue Cheese and Sour Cream Topping
MAKES ENOUGH TO TOP 4 HAMBURGERS
¼ cup (1 ounce) crumbled blue cheese
3 tablespoons sour cream

Gently combine cheese and cream.

Green Garlic Butter
MAKES ENOUGH TO TOP 6 HAMBURGERS
¼ cup butter or margarine, softened
1 medium clove garlic, crushed
1 tablespoon minced chives
1 tablespoon minced parsley
Dash of black pepper

Beat all ingredients until creamy and light.

Pesto Topping
MAKES ENOUGH TO TOP 8 HAMBURGERS
½ cup mayonnaise
¼ cup fresh basil leaves (see note)
¼ cup grated Parmesan or Romano cheese
2 or 3 sprigs of parsley
2 tablespoons coarsely chopped walnuts
1 small clove garlic
Dash of salt

In blender or food processor whirl all ingredients until smooth.

Note: If desired, substitute ⅓ cup parsley sprigs and ½ teaspoon dried basil for fresh basil.

Sautéed Mushrooms in Wine

MAKES ENOUGH TO TOP 4 HAMBURGERS

¼ pound mushrooms, sliced thin (about 1¼ cups)
2 tablespoons butter or margarine
2 tablespoons dry red wine

In medium skillet sauté mushrooms in butter until limp and dry. Add wine; continue cooking until dry.

Open-Faced Cracked Pepper Burgers

SERVES 4

1 pound lean ground beef
2 teaspoons cracked black pepper
1 tablespoon butter or margarine
2 tablespoons brandy
2 hamburger rolls, split and toasted, or 4 thick slices French bread, toasted
⅓ cup heavy cream
1 to 2 teaspoons soy sauce
Chopped parsley

Lightly shape beef in 4 patties and sprinkle ¼ teaspoon pepper on each side. Fry in butter or margarine 2 or 3 minutes on each side or to desired doneness. Pour off fat. Add brandy and flame about 30 seconds; cover with lid to extinguish. Place patties on rolls or bread. Add cream and soy sauce to pan and cook and stir until slightly thickened. Pour over patties and garnish with parsley.

Broiled Hamburger with Blue Cheese on Rye Bread
SERVES 4

1 pound lean ground beef
4 large slices rye bread, toasted on both sides in broiler
  (see note)
Paprika (optional)
Salt and freshly ground pepper to taste
About 2 ounces blue cheese, cut in thin slices

Spread beef on toast to cover completely. Sprinkle lightly with paprika and broil 3 inches from heat about 4 minutes for rare. Season with salt and pepper and top with blue cheese. Serve as is or broil until cheese melts slightly, about 1 minute.

Note: If desired, top sandwiches with another slice of bread.

Reuben-Style Hamburgers
MAKES 4 SANDWICHES

1 pound lean ground beef
Prepared mustard
1 cup drained and rinsed sauerkraut
4 slices Swiss cheese
8 slices rye bread, toasted

Shape beef into 4 oval patties about ¼ inch thick. Spread with mustard and broil on one side only for 3 minutes or to desired doneness. Spread layer of sauerkraut on each patty, top with cheese, and broil until melted. Serve between toast slices.

Stroganoff-Style Hamburgers
SERVES 4

2 tablespoons chopped onion
2 tablespoons butter or margarine
1 pound lean ground beef
¼ pound mushrooms or 3-ounce can sliced or chopped
  mushrooms, drained
Salt and freshly ground black pepper to taste
½ cup sour cream, at room temperature
Chopped parsley (optional)
2 hamburger buns, split, or 4 slices white bread, toasted

Sauté onion in 1 tablespoon butter or margarine until golden;
add to beef. Sauté mushrooms in 1 tablespoon butter or margarine until brown; set aside. Shape beef mixture in 4 patties
and broil 3 to 4 minutes on each side or to desired doneness.
Season with salt and pepper and top with sour cream, mushrooms, and sprinkling of parsley if desired. Serve on bun
halves or toast.

Pizza Burgers
SERVES 4

1 pound lean ground beef
1 teaspoon salt
¼ teaspoon freshly ground black pepper
8-ounce can tomato sauce with onions or mushrooms
4 onion slices
1 teaspoon oregano
2 English muffins, split and toasted
¼ pound mozzarella cheese, sliced

Mix beef, salt, and pepper; shape into four 4-inch patties. Broil
about 3 minutes or each side. Transfer the patties to a shallow

baking dish. Top each with 1 to 2 tablespoons sauce and an onion slice. Sprinkle with oregano. Broil about 1 minute. Place on muffin halves. Top with cheese and broil until cheese is melted.

Tortilla Cheeseburgers
SERVES 8

1 pound lean ground beef
1 small onion, minced
1 small green pepper, minced
8-ounce can tomato sauce
½ teaspoon crushed red pepper
½ teaspoon salt
8 ounces process American cheese slices
8 Flour Tortillas (p. 162) or store-bought

Sauté beef, onion, and green pepper until meat is lightly browned. Add tomato sauce, red pepper, and salt; cook and stir until meat absorbs most of sauce. Place cheese slice on each tortilla; top with meat. Fold 2 sides toward center, then, starting with an unfolded edge, roll up. Serve immediately.

Sloppy Joes in Pita Pockets
MAKES 8 SANDWICHES

1 pound lean ground beef
1 small onion, chopped
½ medium green pepper, diced
16-ounce can tomatoes, chopped
1 tablespoon prepared mustard
2 teaspoons chili powder
1 teaspoon salt
Dash of black pepper
4 loaves Pita, heated and cut in half, or 8 hamburger buns,
    split and toasted

Cook and stir beef, onion, and green pepper until onion is tender. Add tomatoes, mustard, chili powder, salt, and pepper; cover and simmer 15 minutes or until mixture begins to thicken. Spoon into bread pockets or between buns.

Lemon-Rosemary Vealburger
MAKES 4 SANDWICHES

1 pound ground veal
1 egg
¼ cup dry bread crumbs
2 tablespoons grated onion
1 teaspoon grated lemon rind
1 tablespoon lemon juice
¼ teaspoon finely chopped or crushed rosemary
1 teaspoon salt
½ teaspoon freshly ground black pepper
4 crispy round rolls
2 tablespoons Scallion-Mustard Butter

In a bowl combine veal, egg, bread crumbs, onion, lemon rind, lemon juice, rosemary, salt, and pepper. Mix thoroughly to blend. Shape meat into 4 patties. Grill 4 inches from flame in broiler for 5 minutes per side. Slit rolls and spread with seasoned butter; top with vealburger, and then with roll top.

Beef French-Dip
MAKES 4 SANDWICHES

8 to 12 thin slices boiled or roasted beef
1½ to 2 cups beef broth
1 teaspoon Worcestershire sauce
1 large loaf French or Italian bread, split, then cut in quarters, or 4 hero rolls, split

In skillet heat beef in broth with Worcestershire sauce. Remove beef and keep warm. Over high heat stir broth mixture until reduced by half. Dip cut surfaces of bread in broth mixture; place bottom pieces, dipped side up, on plates; top with beef, then spoon on any remaining broth mixture. Cover with top pieces. Serve as is or, if you have additional broth, with ½ to 1 cup per person for dipping sandwich or sipping.

Hot Pot Roast Sandwiches
MAKES 8 SANDWICHES

½ cup reserved pan drippings from Pot Roast (recipe below)
About 1 cup water
About 1 cup beef broth
1 to 1½ pounds Pot Roast, sliced thin
8 thin diagonally cut slices French or Italian bread
Salt and freshly ground black pepper

In large skillet heat drippings and enough water and broth for desired gravy consistency, stirring occasionally. Add meat; heat gently. Spoon some gravy on each bread slice, then top with roast. Spoon on remaining gravy. Season with salt and pepper.

Pot Roast
SERVES ABOUT 16

Slice some pot roast and serve with vegetables (there are enough vegetables for 4 or 5 servings). Cut up remaining roast for sandwiches—you'll have enough for 8 sandwiches.

2 tablespoons flour
2 teaspoons salt
1½ teaspoons thyme
¼ teaspoon freshly ground black pepper
1 small bay leaf, crumbled
5 pounds beef for pot roast (bottom round or rump)
2 tablespoons oil
3 medium onions, quartered
2 large cloves garlic, crushed
6 medium carrots, cut diagonally in 2-inch pieces
6 large ribs celery, halved lengthwise and crosswise
8 small potatoes, peeled (if desired) and halved
About ¾ cup water or beef broth

Mix flour, salt, thyme, pepper, and bay leaf; rub into meat. Heat oil in large skillet with domed vented lid or in Dutch oven. Brown meat slowly on all sides. When browning last side, add onions and garlic; brown lightly. Cover skillet and open vent or leave lid slightly ajar. Simmer about 2 hours, stirring onions once or twice. Add carrots, celery, potatoes, and water. Simmer covered until all is tender, about another hour. (Add a little more water if necessary.)

Remove roast; let rest several minutes before slicing. Slice desired number of servings; arrange on heated platter with vegetables; keep warm. Cover and refrigerate or freeze remaining roast for other uses. If you plan to make Hot Pot Roast Sandwiches, reserve ½ cup drippings; cover and refrigerate. To remaining drippings in pot, add enough water or beef broth to make gravy of desired consistency. Heat gravy well; adjust seasonings. Spoon some over roast and vegetables; pass remainder.

Frankfurters

The frankfurter by any name (wiener, frank, hot dog, or furter) is America's most popular sausage. Frankfurters are made from a number of different meats and other ingredients. The package label must list the ingredients. Kosher franks are produced under rabbinical supervision.

Frankfurters are fully cooked and smoked and may be eaten without further cooking; however, heating enhances their flavor.

Most frankfurters are packed 10 to the pound; some, 8 to the pound.

Frankfurters are nutritious. One all-beef frankfurter supplies about 7 grams protein and 10 grams fat and is high in B vitamins. It contains about 124 calories. Frankfurters are fairly high in fat, but cannot contain more than 30 percent.

Skinless frankfurters are cooked, smoked, and chilled in the casing, then the casing is removed, producing especially tender frankfurters.

You can store opened packages of frankfurters in the refrigerator up to one week, in the freezer up to two months.

To simmer: Place in small amount of boiling water, reduce heat, cover, and simmer about 5 minutes or until heated through. Do not boil.

To panbroil: Place in cold skillet over medium heat; turn often with tongs until of desired brownness.

To pan-fry: Use a small amount of butter or fat over medium heat, turning often with tongs until of desired brownness.

To broil or grill: Place about 4 inches from heat 6 to 8 minutes; turn once or twice to brown evenly.

To heat in microwave oven: Wrap individually in paper napkin or arrange in shallow glass baking dish. Heat 2 frankfurters 1 minute 15 seconds; 5 frankfurters (½ pound) 2 minutes 30 seconds; 10 frankfurters (1 pound) 5 minutes.

Frankfurters with Peppers and Onion
MAKES 8 TO 10 SANDWICHES

2 green peppers, halved and sliced
2 ribs celery, sliced thin
1 large onion, halved and sliced
2 tablespoons oil
1 pound frankfurters, slit
Prepared mustard
8 to 10 frankfurter rolls
Butter or margarine
2 tablespoons sesame seeds

Sauté peppers, celery, and onion in oil until tender; set aside.
Spread frankfurters with mustard and broil until browned.
Spread cut sides of rolls with butter or margarine, sprinkle
with sesame seeds, and toast under broiler. Put frankfurter in
each roll and top with pepper mixture.

Frankfurters with Special Sauerkraut
MAKES 8 TO 10 SANDWICHES

1 pound sauerkraut
2 scallions with tops, sliced
½ teaspoon caraway seeds
½ cup water
1 pound frankfurters
8 to 10 frankfurter rolls
Prepared mustard

In a skillet heat sauerkraut, scallions, caraway seeds, and
water. Cover and simmer for 10 minutes, adding additional

water if necessary. Top with frankfurters and cook until hot, about 5 minutes. Serve in warmed rolls with mustard.

Mustard Franks Parmesan
MAKES 8 TO 10 SANDWICHES

8 to 10 slices soft white bread
About ½ cup butter or margarine, melted
Prepared mustard
1 pound frankfurters
¼ cup Parmesan cheese

Flatten bread slices with rolling pin, brush with some of the butter or margarine, then spread with mustard. Place a frankfurter on each bread slice and roll tightly. Place seam side down on greased jelly-roll pan, drizzle with remaining butter, and sprinkle with cheese. Bake in preheated 450° F. oven 10 to 12 minutes or until crisp and browned.

Frankfurters with Onion Chili Sauce
MAKES 4 SANDWICHES

1 cup minced onion
½ teaspoon minced garlic, or to taste
¼ cup butter or margarine
½ teaspoon salt
¼ teaspoon black pepper
1½ teaspoons Worcestershire sauce
1½ tablespoons prepared mustard
1½ teaspoons light brown sugar
½ cup bottled chili sauce
8 frankfurters
Four 6-inch Italian hard rolls

Cook onion and garlic in butter or margarine until golden. Add salt, pepper, Worcestershire sauce, mustard, sugar, and chili sauce. Simmer for 5 minutes, adding 1 tablespoon of water if sauce gets too thick. Split frankfurters almost all the way through lengthwise and add to sauce. Simmer 5 minutes more. Split rolls lengthwise almost all the way through and toast under a broiler until golden. Serve 2 frankfurters on each roll and spoon sauce over.

Frankfurter-Sauerkraut Roll-Ups
MAKES 8 SANDWICHES

3 cups all-purpose buttermilk biscuit mix
⅔ cup water
About 1 tablespoon flour
8 frankfurters
Prepared mustard
¾ cup sauerkraut, drained, washed, and heated through

In a small bowl combine buttermilk biscuit mix with water. Stir with fork to form a soft dough. Form into a ball, transfer to lightly floured surface, and knead five or so turns. Divide dough in two. Roll each portion into a 12-inch circle and cut each in four wedges. Spread each wedge with mustard and 1 tablespoon of sauerkraut. Put a frankfurter on each wedge and roll up, beginning at wide end. Put on greased baking sheet and bake in 450° F. oven about 15 minutes. Serve hot or at room temperature.

Bacon-Cheese Dogs
MAKES 8 TO 10 SANDWICHES

4 or 5 slices bacon, cut in half
1 pound frankfurters
3 slices process American cheese, chopped
8 to 10 frankfurter rolls, toasted
Catsup or prepared mustard

Broil bacon 1 to 2 minutes until partially cooked. Slit frankfurters and fill with cheese; wrap with bacon and broil, cheese side up, until lightly browned. Serve in rolls with catsup or mustard.

Crusty Corn Dogs
MAKES 8 TO 10 SANDWICHES

Flour
¼ cup cornmeal
¼ teaspoon salt
¼ teaspoon baking soda
½ cup buttermilk
1 egg
1 pound frankfurters
Oil for deep frying
Mustard or catsup

Mix ½ cup flour, the cornmeal, salt, and baking soda. Beat together buttermilk and egg, then stir into flour mixture until smooth. Cut frankfurters in half crosswise; insert wood skewer lengthwise in each piece, then roll in flour to coat. Dip in cornmeal batter to coat. Fry in about 2 inches hot oil (370° F. on deep-fat thermometer), 2 to 3 minutes or until golden brown. Drain on paper towels. Serve hot with mustard or catsup.

Hot Corned Beef on Rye with Mustard Sauce
MAKES 4 SANDWICHES

¼ to ½ cup beef broth
¾ to 1 pound thinly sliced cooked corned beef
4 to 8 slices rye bread
Mustard Sauce (recipe below or ½ cup bought)
Sauerkraut (optional)

Heat broth in skillet until hot. Add corned beef, cover, and steam until hot, about 2 minutes. Spread 4 slices bread with Mustard Sauce, top with corned beef, and drizzle with more sauce to taste. Serve sandwiches open-faced or top with another slice of bread, if desired. Cut in halves. Good with heated sauerkraut.

Mustard Sauce
MAKES ABOUT ½ CUP
In small bowl with small whisk beat together 3 tablespoons prepared mustard, 2 tablespoons each sugar and cider vinegar, and 1 teaspoon dry mustard. Pour in ¼ cup oil slowly while beating; beat until sauce is smooth, shiny, and thickened.

Sausage Patties and Tomatoes Provençal on a Muffin
SERVES 2

Four 2-ounce pork sausage patties
2 English muffins
2 small tomatoes
1 small clove garlic, crushed or very finely minced
4 teaspoons olive oil
½ teaspoon oregano
¼ cup fine bread crumbs

Sauté sausage patties in frying pan over medium-low heat until brown on both sides and cooked through. Split and toast English muffin halves under broiler. When patties are cooked, place on muffin halves. Slice tomatoes into 4 thick slices and place on top of sausage patties. Sauté garlic in olive oil for just a few seconds and then add oregano and bread crumbs and stir to mix thoroughly. Sprinkle crumbs over tomatoes and grill under broiler for a few minutes until crumbs are browned and tomatoes warmed.

Sausage Patties on Raisin Toast
MAKES 2 SANDWICHES

Four 2-ounce pork sausage patties
4 slices raisin bread, toasted
¼ cup apple butter
2 leaves Boston lettuce

Sauté sausage patties in a frying pan over medium-low heat until golden brown on both sides and cooked through. Spread all 4 slices of raisin toast with apple butter, cut patties in half, and arrange on top of toast. Top with lettuce leaves and remaining toast slices.

Fried Bologna on Whole Wheat Bread
MAKES 1 SANDWICH

This hearty snack is a great after-school favorite—or midnight treat after study.

2 teaspoons butter or margarine
2 slices bologna
Prepared mustard
2 slices whole wheat bread
Thinly sliced dill pickles

In a small skillet melt butter or margarine over medium-high flame. Add bologna and sauté quickly until brown on both sides. Spread mustard on one slice of bread; add bologna, pickle slices, and then remaining piece of bread.

French-Toasted Ham and Cheese
MAKES 4 SANDWICHES

1 egg
¼ cup milk
8 slices whole wheat bread
4 slices Edam or Gouda cheese
4 slices ham
Butter or margarine

In pie plate or other shallow dish, beat together egg and milk. Make 4 sandwiches with bread, cheese, and ham; dip both sides in egg mixture. Grill in hot well-buttered griddle or skillet over medium heat until golden brown on both sides. Serve at once.

Ham Soufflé on Toast
MAKES 4 SANDWICHES

2 eggs, separated
½ cup chopped cooked ham
½ teaspoon Worcestershire sauce
½ cup shredded Cheddar cheese
1 tablespoon mayonnaise
1 tablespoon chopped scallions or parsley
½ teaspoon salt
4 slices white bread, toasted

Beat the egg yolks until thick. Add the ham, Worcestershire sauce, cheese, mayonnaise, and scallions or parsley. Beat the egg whites with the salt until stiff, and fold them into the yolk mixture. Place toast on a baking pan and pile the egg-cheese mixture lightly on the toast. Heat under broiler until puffy and lightly browned.

Note: You may substitute chopped sautéed mushrooms for the ham.

Grilled Cheese and Ham on Rye Bread
MAKES **4** SANDWICHES

8 slices Sour Rye Bread
Butter or margarine, softened
Prepared mustard
8 slices process American, Swiss, or Cheddar cheese
    (about ½ pound)
8 slices cooked ham (about ½ pound)

Spread 4 slices bread with butter or margarine and 4 slices with mustard. Place cheese, then ham, on buttered bread; top with remaining bread. Cut in halves diagonally. Grill sandwiches in small amount of butter in skillet or on griddle over medium heat until golden, about 3 minutes on each side.

Barbecued Ham in Pita Pockets
MAKES 6 SANDWICHES

1 tablespoon oil
2½ cups shredded cooked smoked ham
½ cup diced green pepper
1 small onion, diced
8-ounce can tomato sauce
2 tablespoons packed brown sugar
2 tablespoons vinegar
1 tablespoon chili powder
1 teaspoon dry mustard
⅛ teaspoon black pepper
3 loaves Pita or 6 split and toasted hamburger buns

In large skillet heat oil and sauté ham, green pepper, and onion until lightly browned. Stir in tomato sauce, sugar, vinegar, chili powder, mustard, and pepper; simmer 10 minutes. Meanwhile warm pita loaves in oven. Cut pita in half and with fingers spread pocket open in each half and spoon in ham mixture. Or fill hamburger buns.

Baked Broccoli and Chicken on Crusty Bread
MAKES 4 SANDWICHES

1 loaf Italian or French bread
Mayonnaise
¾ pound fresh or 10-ounce package frozen broccoli, cut in
    3-inch pieces, cooked, and well drained
¾ pound sliced cooked chicken or turkey
⅔ cup packed coarsely shredded Cheddar cheese
2 tablespoons chicken broth or milk

Split bread lengthwise and place cut side up on cookie sheet. Cut each in 4 diagonal pieces; spread with mayonnaise. Arrange broccoli on bottom pieces and chicken or turkey on top pieces. Stir together ½ cup mayonnaise, the cheese, and broth or milk until well blended. Spoon or spread over broccoli and chicken. Bake in preheated 425° F. oven until bubbly and golden brown, about 10 minutes.

Chicken Livers and Mushrooms on Toast
SERVES 4

¾ pound chicken livers, halved
2 tablespoons flour
¾ teaspoon salt
¼ teaspoon basil
⅛ teaspoon black pepper
2 tablespoons minced scallions
2 cups sliced mushrooms
3 tablespoons butter or margarine
¼ cup heavy cream or half-and-half (optional)
4 to 8 slices bread, toasted
Chopped parsley

Drain livers on paper towels, then coat with mixture of flour, salt, basil, and pepper; set aside. Sauté scallions and mushrooms in 1 tablespoon butter or margarine in skillet over medium heat until tender, about 4 minutes, stirring occasionally; remove mushrooms and scallions and reserve. Melt remaining 2 tablespoons butter or margarine in skillet, add livers, and sauté until of desired doneness, about 5 minutes. Return mushrooms and onion to skillet, stir in cream (if you like), and heat. Spoon mushroom-liver mixture on toast and sprinkle with parsley.

Turkey, Mushrooms, and Mozzarella on Sesame Whole Wheat Bread

MAKES 2 SANDWICHES

Whenever you have turkey leftovers (or when your supermarket is offering a special on turkey breasts), these festive sandwiches are a delightful way to serve roast turkey.

1 to 2 tablespoons butter or margarine
¼ pound fresh mushrooms
¼ teaspoon dried marjoram
Salt and black pepper to taste
4 slices Sesame Whole Wheat Bread
1 tablespoon mayonnaise
4 to 6 slices roast turkey breast
¼ pound mozzarella cheese, sliced

In a small frying pan melt butter or margarine and sauté mushrooms for just a few minutes until golden. Season mushrooms with marjoram, salt, and pepper. Toast bread. Spread 2 slices of bread lightly with mayonnaise, put on turkey slices and mushrooms, then top with mozzarella. Grill under broiler until cheese is melted. Add remaining bread slices.

Open-Faced Turkey Barbecue on a Bun
SERVES 6

16-ounce can tomatoes, cut up
½ cup beer
2 tablespoons minced onion
2 tablespoons Worcestershire sauce
2 tablespoons brown sugar
1 tablespoon dry mustard
1 to 2 teaspoons chili powder
½ teaspoon salt
Black pepper to taste
2 cups coarsely chopped cooked turkey
6 hamburger buns, split and toasted

In medium skillet combine tomatoes, beer, onion, Worcester-shire sauce, sugar, mustard, chili powder, salt, and pepper. Simmer 30 minutes, then add turkey and heat well. Just before serving, spoon over bun halves.

Broiled Sardine and Egg on Pumpernickel Bread
MAKES 8 SANDWICHES

8 slices pumpernickel or other bread
⅓ cup mayonnaise
4 hard-cooked eggs, sliced
Salt and black pepper
Two 3¾-ounce cans sardines, drained
Dillweed
1 lemon, cut in 8 wedges

Toast one side of bread in broiler; turn and spread thinly with mayonnaise. Arrange about 4 slices egg on half of each slice of bread. Season lightly with salt and pepper. Place 2 sardines next to egg. Broil about 3 inches from heat 3 minutes or until sardines are hot. Put dollop of mayonnaise on center of each sandwich and sprinkle with dillweed. Serve with lemon wedges.

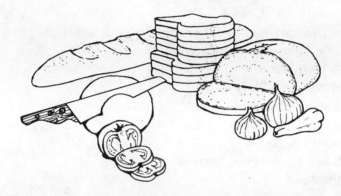

Fish on a Bun with Green Sauce
MAKES 4 SANDWICHES

8 ounces fried fish fillets or fish portions
4 hamburger buns, split and toasted
Green Sauce (recipe below)
4 tomato slices
Lemon wedges (optional)

Cook fish, following package directions. Place on bottom halves of buns. Spread with about 1 tablespoon Green Sauce. Add tomato slices and bun tops. Serve with lemon wedges and, if desired, additional Green Sauce.

Green Sauce
MAKES ABOUT 1 CUP

In blender whirl until smooth 1 cup mayonnaise, ½ cup packed fresh parsley leaves, 2 teaspoons sweet pickle relish, and 1 scallion, cut in chunks. Season with salt and black pepper to taste. Will keep in refrigerator about 1 week.

French-Toasted Tuna on White Bread
MAKES 4 SANDWICHES

9¼-ounce can tuna, drained and flaked
¾ cup minced celery
2 scallions, minced
¼ cup mayonnaise (or enough to bind salad)
1 to 2 teaspoons prepared mustard
½ teaspoon salt
⅛ teaspoon black pepper
8 slices firm white bread
2 eggs
¼ cup milk
2 to 3 tablespoons butter or margarine
Pickles

Combine tuna, celery, scallions, mayonnaise, mustard, salt, and pepper in mixing bowl. Stir with fork until blended and of spreading consistency. Spread on 4 slices of bread; top with remaining bread. Cut each sandwich in half diagonally. In pie plate beat eggs with milk until well blended. Dip sandwich halves in egg mixture, turning to moisten both sides. Fry in hot butter or margarine in skillet until golden brown and crisp on both sides. Serve warm with pickles.

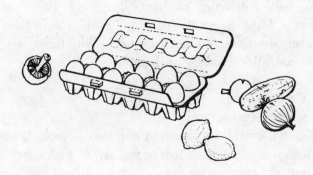

Broiled Tuna Rolls

MAKES 4 SANDWICHES

6½- or 7-ounce can tuna, flaked
1 cup chopped celery
¼ cup mayonnaise
1 tablespoon chopped scallion or onion
1 to 2 teaspoons prepared mustard
¼ teaspoon salt
⅛ teaspoon black pepper
4 hamburger rolls, split and toasted, or 8 slices toast
Grated Parmesan to taste

In bowl mix all ingredients except rolls and Parmesan. Place roll bottoms or 4 slices of toast on cookie sheet; spread with tuna mixture to cover. Sprinkle with Parmesan; broil about 6 inches from heat source until bubbly, about 5 minutes. Cover with roll tops or remaining slices of toast; cut each sandwich in half.

Broiled Crab Meat and Cheese on Whole Wheat Bread

SERVES 4

8 slices whole wheat bread
Two 3-ounce packages cream cheese, softened
2 tablespoons chopped scallions
2 tablespoons milk
6 ounces frozen crab meat, thawed, drained, and flaked
¼ cup mayonnaise
1 teaspoon lemon juice
1 teaspoon Worcestershire sauce
Dash of hot pepper sauce
Buttered bread crumbs

Toast bread on one side in broiler. Combine cream cheese, scallions, and milk and stir to combine thoroughly. In a small bowl combine crab meat, mayonnaise, lemon juice, Worcestershire sauce, and pepper sauce and stir to mix thoroughly. Spread the cheese mixture on untoasted sides of bread, top with crab mixture, and then with buttered crumbs. Bake in preheated 350° F. oven 5 to 10 minutes until heated through.

Cheese and Green Chilies on Sourdough Bread
MAKES 4 SANDWICHES

Butter
8 large slices sourdough bread
Four 1-ounce slices Monterey Jack or mozzarella cheese
4-ounce can green chilies, or 2 fresh mild green chilies, sliced

Butter bread lightly and put a slice of cheese and some slices of chili on 4 pieces. Top with remaining bread, also lightly buttered. Grill on a greased griddle until bread is browned and turn to brown other side.

Italian Cheese Loaf
MAKES 4 SANDWICHES

1 large loaf Italian or French bread
3 tablespoons butter or margarine, melted
¼ teaspoon oregano or 1 teaspoon chopped fresh basil
½ pound mozzarella, Swiss, or Monterey Jack cheese, sliced
Several thin slices tomato
Several thin slices red or other mild onion (optional)

Cut bread in ½-inch slices almost to bottom, being careful not to cut all the way through. Mix butter or margarine and oregano or basil; brush between first 2 slices of bread, skip a slice, then brush between next 2 slices and so on to end of loaf. Divide and insert cheese, tomato, and onion slices between buttered slices. Bake on a cookie sheet in preheated 350° F. oven 20 to 30 minutes or until cheese is melted. To serve, cut between unfilled slices.

Broiled Pineapple-Cheese on Wheat Bread
SERVES 4

8 slices wheatberry bread, toasted
2½ cups small-curd cottage cheese
Two 8-ounce cans sliced pineapple in juice, drained
Cinnamon

Spread toast with cottage cheese. Top each portion with pineapple slice and sprinkle with cinnamon. Broil about 6 inches from heat source for 4 or 5 minutes or until hot.

4 ▸ AMERICA'S REGIONAL BOUNTY

IF YOU WERE TO DRIVE ACROSS THE LENGTH AND BREADTH OF THE United States you would soon discover that every region of the country has its own much-loved sandwich favorites. On the highways of coastal New England you would see bright signs advertising succulent Fried Clam Rolls, in Philadelphia competing sandwich shops would lay claim to the best Steak Sandwiches in the city, and all through the Southeast roadside restaurants would urge you to sample their Pork Barbecue. And after only one day in New Orleans you'd know that that city's great favorites are Oyster Loaves and the long-popular Roast Beef Poor Boys, a very special New Orleans version of the hero. A visit to Texas would assure you that the Lone Star State is crazy about Chili Dogs. While out in California the people's choice is often a happy combination of Monterey Jack cheese, sprouts, avocado, and tomato. Although we may be a nation of hamburger lovers, it's also true that in every state of the Union imaginative cooks have created memorable sandwiches from their region's bounty.

To introduce you to the best of these specialties, we have

102

gathered together a sampling of authentic regional recipes that you can enjoy no matter where you live. Some of these may require a bit more effort than ordinary sandwiches, but we think that once you taste them you'll agree that they are well worth the extra time and care. Here is a wonderful opportunity to take a food lover's tour of America.

New England Lobster Roll
MAKES 4 SANDWICHES

At first thought, the idea of serving lobster salad on a roll may strike you as extravagant, but it's a wonderful way to stretch lobster meat. And if you serve these with a crisp green salad, slices of melon, and iced tea, they make a delightful weekend party lunch.

1½ cups cooked lobster meat
¼ cup vinaigrette dressing, made from olive oil and tarragon vinegar
¾ cup finely diced celery
2 teaspoons finely chopped scallions
½ cup Blender Mayonnaise
1 tablespoon finely chopped parsley
Freshly ground black pepper to taste
4 frankfurter rolls
2 to 3 tablespoons melted butter

Combine lobster meat with vinaigrette and marinate for an hour. Next add celery, scallions, mayonnaise, parsley, and pepper and stir to mix thoroughly. Toast frankfurter buns in broiler, brush them lightly with butter, and fill with equal portions of lobster salad.

Fried Clam Roll
MAKES 1 SANDWICH

Crisp golden fried clams on a frankfurter roll are one of the great treats of the summer in coastal New England. Some roadside stands sell only these and cold drinks. You can use either steamers or hardshell clams, but if clams are large slice them in two or three pieces before cooking. These sandwiches are often accompanied by a small portion of coleslaw or sliced beefsteak tomatoes on Boston lettuce.

6 to 8 clams
1 egg, mixed with 3 tablespoons water
½ cup fine dry bread crumbs, seasoned with salt and black
  pepper
Vegetable oil for deep frying
1 frankfurter bun
Tartar Sauce

If you are using steamers, remove the necks and wash very carefully to remove sand. Place the clams between sheets of waxed paper and roll with rolling pin to flatten. If you are using hardshell clams (either littlenecks or cherrystones, which are slightly larger), simply drain opened clams in a colander. Dip the opened clams in the egg-water mixture and then in the seasoned bread crumbs, making sure to coat them well. Let the breaded clams stand on a sheet of waxed paper or foil to dry. Heat oil to 375° F. (use a candy thermometer to gauge heat) and fry clams for about 3 minutes until golden brown. Drain on paper towels. Fill toasted frankfurter bun with clams and serve tartar sauce on the side.

Boston Baked Bean Sandwiches
MAKES 4 SANDWICHES

Bean sandwiches? Yes, indeed. These were invented by thrifty New England housewives to make use of leftover home-baked beans, but now they're popular just because they taste so good. When you bake your own New England–style beans, do use any leftovers for this recipe, but you can also make delicious sandwiches from canned baked beans.

> 8 slices Baked Applesauce Brown Bread or canned brown bread
> 2 tablespoons butter or margarine
> 1½ to 2 cups (or 1-pound can) Boston-style baked beans
> Coleslaw (recipe below)

Spread 4 slices of bread with butter or margarine and then top with generous portion of beans (drain in slotted spoon if you are using canned beans). Add a generous layer of coleslaw over the beans and close with remaining slices of bread.

Coleslaw
MAKES ABOUT 2 CUPS
1½ cups finely shredded cabbage
¼ green pepper, seeded and finely sliced
¼ small onion, finely chopped
⅓ cup mayonnaise
Salt and black pepper to taste

Combine all ingredients and chill for 1 to 2 hours. Drain before adding to sandwiches.

Reuben Sandwiches
MAKES 4 SANDWICHES

You can find these all across the country now. We even had one once on a palm-fringed Caribbean island. But the first of these tangy sandwiches was created by New York's famous Reuben's Restaurant.

8 slices Sour Rye Bread
⅓ cup Russian Dressing
½ pound sliced lean cooked corned beef
1 pound sauerkraut, rinsed and well drained
½ pound sliced Swiss cheese
Softened butter or margarine

Spread 4 slices of bread with Russian dressing and for each sandwich arrange a layer of corned beef, a layer of sauerkraut (about ¼ to ⅓ cup), and a layer of cheese. Lightly butter the remaining 4 slices of bread and top the sandwiches. Spread both sides of outside of sandwich with butter and brown on a grill or in a hot frying pan until golden and cheese has melted.

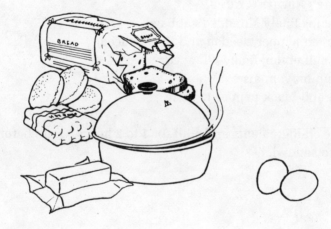

Grilled Sausage, Peppers, and Onions on a Hero
MAKES 4 SANDWICHES

In New York's Little Italy the tempting aroma of grilled sausages, peppers, and onions permeates the air at street fairs and in sandwich shops. A longtime favorite, this robust combination served on crusty loaves of Italian bread is sometimes the only sandwich offered by small cafés and pizza parlors.

2 tablespoons vegetable oil
6 Italian-style pork sausages, sweet or hot
2 onions, sliced
2 or 3 green peppers, seeded and sliced
Salt and freshly ground black pepper
Two 12-inch loaves Italian bread, cut in half

In a frying pan heat 1 tablespoon oil and cook sausages over medium-high heat until brown and cooked through, 20 to 25 minutes. In another frying pan, heat 1 tablespoon oil and sauté onions and green peppers until onions are limp and golden, but not brown, and peppers are heated through and crisp-tender. Season to taste with salt and pepper. Heat bread in 350° F. oven until crisp and warm, 4 to 5 minutes. Slice bread lengthwise to open, without separating top and bottom pieces. Place 1½ sausages on each 6-inch length of bread and cover with onion-pepper mixture.

Meatball Heroes
MAKES 4 SANDWICHES

Here is another of the memorable sandwiches served in the Italian-American sandwich shops of New York.

1 pound lean ground beef
¼ cup finely chopped onion
¼ cup water
1 small clove garlic, finely minced
½ teaspoon dried oregano
¾ teaspoon salt
¼ teaspoon black pepper
½ cup fine dry bread crumbs
2 tablespoons vegetable oil
2 medium green peppers, seeded and sliced
15½-ounce jar spaghetti sauce
4 hero or French rolls or larger Italian loaves cut into 6-
   inch lengths
Dried crushed red pepper
Grated Parmesan cheese

Mix beef, onion, water, garlic, oregano, salt, and pepper; add
bread crumbs and combine thoroughly. Shape into 12 meatballs about 1½ inches in diameter. Brown meatballs in hot oil,
remove, and set aside. Add green pepper to drippings in skillet
and sauté until lightly browned. Drain excess fat. Add spaghetti sauce and meatballs; cover and simmer 15 minutes. Heat
rolls a few minutes in 350° F. oven, then slit lengthwise a little
more than halfway. Place 3 meatballs on each roll and spoon
sauce over them. Serve with dried crushed red pepper and
grated Parmesan cheese for extra seasoning.

Philadelphia Steak Sandwiches
MAKES 2 SANDWICHES

As any food-loving native of Philadelphia will tell you, there's
an art to making the perfect steak sandwich. The most important thing is to start with very thin slices of raw beef sirloin or
flank steak. (One good way to get really thin slices is to partially freeze the meat before slicing.) These are quick to make

and thoroughly delightful. A simple variation called a Cheese Steak is another favorite in the City of Brotherly Love.

> Two 6-inch Italian or French loaves
> 2 tablespoons vegetable oil
> ½ to ¾ pound beef sirloin or flank steak, sliced very thin
> 2 medium onions, sliced thin
> Salt and black pepper
> 1 or 2 teaspoons oil (optional)
> Two 1-ounce slices American cheese (optional)
> Pickled cherry peppers or hot pepper sauce (optional)

Warm bread in 350° F. oven for about 5 minutes. In a heavy-bottomed frying pan heat oil and quickly sauté beef until just brown. Slice bread in half lengthwise. Spoon meat onto bottom halves. Briefly sauté onions in same pan, seasoning with salt and pepper. (Add a little more oil if necessary.) Top beef with onions. If using cheese, add that now and melt it quickly under broiler. Replace tops of bread. If desired, serve with pickled cherry peppers or hot pepper sauce.

Delaware Chicken Shortcake
SERVES 4

Delaware is famous for its great chicken dishes. This one is so good it's been adopted by many other parts of the country. Make it for a festive Sunday brunch or supper.

> 3½ tablespoons butter or margarine
> 2½ tablespoons all-purpose flour
> 2 cups rich chicken broth
> Salt and black pepper to taste
> Pinch of poultry seasoning
> ½ pound fresh mushrooms, sliced
> 2½ cups cooked chicken, cut into large dice
> 8 buttermilk biscuits, made from mix

In a small frying pan melt 2½ tablespoons butter or margarine. Add flour, whisk to blend, and cook over medium heat a few minutes. Add chicken broth, stirring as you pour, and cook until thick. Season with salt, pepper, and poultry seasoning. In another small frying pan, melt the remaining 1 tablespoon butter or margarine and sauté mushrooms, turning to brown lightly on both sides. Add to sauce. Stir in chicken and heat through. Split biscuits and serve chicken over them.

Baltimore Crab Cakes on a Bun
MAKES 2 SANDWICHES

Some Baltimore cooks make these without the bread crumbs, but we have found the crumbs help to bind the mixture. Either way these are extraordinary.

> Fresh bread crumbs from 1 slice white bread
> ½ cup milk
> ½ pound crab meat
> ½ teaspoon dry mustard
> ½ teaspoon white pepper
> 1 teaspoon Worcestershire sauce
> Salt to taste
> 1 egg yolk
> 1 teaspoon mayonnaise
> ½ teaspoon chopped parsley
> ½ cup all-purpose flour
> 1 egg, beaten with 1 tablespoon water
> ½ cup dry bread crumbs
> 2 tablespoons vegetable oil
> 2 hamburger buns

Mix fresh bread crumbs and milk, then squeeze to remove excess milk. Combine crumbs, crab meat, mustard, pepper, and Worcestershire sauce. Taste, and add salt if necessary. Add egg yolk, mayonnaise, and parsley and mix to combine thoroughly.

Form crab mixture into 2 large, flat cakes. Coat cakes with flour; dip in egg-water mixture and then in crumbs. Fry in hot oil over medium-high heat, turning to brown on both sides. Serve on toasted buns.

Barbecued Pork on a Bun
MAKES 8 TO 10 SANDWICHES

Most places in the South, where it's a great favorite in roadside restaurants, this is simply called "barbecue."

1½ cups water
¼ cup cider vinegar
¼ cup light brown sugar
4 teaspoons prepared mustard
2 teaspoons salt
⅛ to ¼ teaspoon ground red pepper
2 slices lemon
1 onion, chopped
¼ cup vegetable oil
4 cups shredded cooked pork roast or braised pork shoulder
1 cup catsup
1 tablespoon Worcestershire sauce
8 to 10 hamburger buns

In a large saucepan combine water, vinegar, sugar, mustard, salt, red pepper, lemon, onion, and oil. Simmer uncovered for 15 to 20 minutes. Add pork, catsup, and Worcestershire sauce. Simmer slowly for 30 minutes. Serve on hamburger buns.

Oyster Loaf
MAKES 4 SANDWICHES

If you're an oyster lover, try this treat from New Orleans, and we think you'll agree it's one of the world's best sandwiches.

    2 dozen oysters, shucked
    2 eggs
    ½ cup milk
    ½ teaspoon salt
    ½ teaspoon freshly ground black pepper
    2 cups stone-ground cornmeal
    Two 12- or 13-inch loaves French or Italian bread, cut in
        half
    4 tablespoons butter, melted
    Vegetable oil for deep frying
    Tartar Sauce (optional)

Drain the oysters. In a small bowl whisk eggs and milk until well blended. Mix salt and pepper with the cornmeal and spread it out on a plate or a piece of foil. Dip the oysters, one at a time, in the egg mixture and then in the cornmeal, making sure to coat them completely. When all the oysters are coated arrange them on a plate and chill for about an hour. Slice each half loaf of bread horizontally. Pull away some of the doughy center of the bread and, with a pastry brush, brush insides of loaf with butter. Place on cookie sheet or foil and warm in 350° F. oven for about 5 minutes. Heat the oil in a deep fryer and when it is 375° F. fry the oysters 6 at a time for 3 or 4 minutes until golden brown. Transfer oysters to paper towel to drain, and fry another 6 oysters. Put 6 oysters on bottom of one sandwich, spread top with tartar sauce if desired, and cover oysters with top. Repeat until all the oyster loaves are assembled.

Muffuletta
MAKES 4 AVERAGE SERVINGS OR 2 GENEROUS SERVINGS

This delectable garlic-scented sandwich was created by two Italian specialty stores in the French Quarter of New Orleans. It's a big sandwich, and usually one half is considered a serving. But once you've eaten your first half, you may regret giving the other half away.

> 2 loaves round Italian bread (8 to 10 inches across)
> 9¾-ounce jar olive condite (Italian marinated olive salad; see note)
> 1 large clove garlic
> ¼ to ½ pound Genoa salami, thinly sliced
> ¼ to ½ pound mortadella (see note)
> ¼ to ½ pound provolone cheese, thinly sliced
> ¼ to ½ pound boiled ham, thinly sliced

Slice loaves in half horizontally. Brush bottom halves with olive oil from olive salad and then rub with cut garlic clove. Place half the salami and half the mortadella on one loaf and half on the other; top with cheese, and then with ham. Add a layer of olive salad. Brush tops of loaves with oil and rub with garlic. Cut in half and serve. Or first warm the loaves in a 350° F. oven for 5 to 8 minutes, then cut and serve.

Note: Since the olive condite is the secret of this sandwich, it has to be used. If you cannot find it in an Italian specialty store, you can make your own. Combine 1 cup coarsely chopped pimiento olives, 1 cup pitted Greek or Italian green olives, 2 tablespoons capers, ½ cup finely sliced celery, ¼ cup olive oil, 1 tablespoon red wine vinegar, and ½ teaspoon oregano. Marinate at least 24 hours.

Mortadella is a bologna-like sausage available in Italian specialty stores and some gourmet markets.

Roast Beef Poor Boys

MAKES 8 SANDWICHES

Although these sandwiches are called "Roast" Beef, they are actually made from pot roasted beef. "Poor Boy" is the New Orleans name for a "hero," "grinder," "hoagie," "wedge," or "submarine." Whatever you call them, these are unforgettable.

> Four 12-inch-long loaves of crisp French bread
> Mayonnaise
> 1 large head iceberg lettuce, thinly shredded
> 3 pounds Pot Roasted Beef (recipe below), thinly sliced
> 4 medium tomatoes, thinly sliced
> Salt and black pepper

Divide loaves in half and then slice horizontally. Remove some of the doughy part and warm bread in 350° F. oven for 5 minutes. Spread mayonnaise on the bottom half of bread, cover with a layer of shredded lettuce, a layer of thin slices of beef, and a generous portion of gravy. Cover with 3 to 4 slices tomato, salt and pepper, and tops of loaves. Serve immediately.

Pot Roasted Beef
> 2 tablespoons vegetable oil
> 3 pounds chuck or shoulder pot roast
> 1 teaspoon salt
> ½ teaspoon black pepper
> 1 small onion
> ½ cup water

In a Dutch oven, heat oil and brown meat on all sides. Remove meat and put rack in kettle. Place meat on rack and season with salt and pepper. Add onion and water and bring water to a boil. Lower heat, cover, and simmer the pot roast for 2 to 3 hours until tender. Add another ½ cup water, if necessary to provide enough gravy, so that sandwiches may be generously moistened. Remove meat and skim the fat from liquid. Serve gravy as is or thicken just a little with flour and water (combine 1 tablespoon flour with 2 tablespoons cold water, add to pot, and simmer for a few minutes).

Texas Chili Dogs
MAKES 8 SANDWICHES

This zesty combination of hot dogs and chili (without beans) was invented in Texas, but Americans everywhere are now enthusiastic fans of this great treat. If you make real Texas chili with green chilies, you will capture the authentic Lone Star taste.

    8 frankfurters
    8 frankfurter buns
    Chili (recipe below)

Simmer frankfurters in water for 5 to 6 minutes until heated through. Wrap buns in foil and warm in 350° F. oven for 5 minutes. Place frankfurters in buns and spoon chili over them.

Chili
    ½ pound ground chuck
    ½ clove garlic, minced
    1 small onion, chopped
    1 tablespoon vegetable oil (optional)
    8-ounce can tomatoes
    ½ teaspoon salt
    1 teaspoon chili powder, or more to taste
    ¼ teaspoon oregano
    1 canned green chili, seeded and chopped fine, or ¼ teaspoon crushed red pepper

Combine beef, garlic, and onion in a heavy frying pan and cook slowly over medium-low heat for 10 minutes (if beef sticks add vegetable oil). When beef is brown and onion soft, add tomatoes, salt, chili powder, oregano, and green chili. Simmer for 15 to 20 minutes longer.

Beef Tacos
MAKES 12 SANDWICHES

In California and other western states people can get pretty serious about what goes into a perfect taco. You always start with corn tortillas—in the United States these are folded and deep-fried—and then add a wide variety of spicy fillings and garnishes. Beef, chicken, and cheese are the great favorites. We've cast our vote for beef.

1 pound lean ground beef
1 large onion, chopped (1 cup)
1 large green pepper, chopped (1 cup)
28-ounce can stewed tomatoes
1½ cups water
12-ounce can tomato paste
About 2 teaspoons chili powder
1½ teaspoons salt
1½ teaspoons ground coriander
1 teaspoon cumin
½ teaspoon thyme
½ teaspoon oregano
2 teaspoons wine vinegar
½ ounce (½ square) unsweetened chocolate
1 large clove garlic, crushed
16-ounce can red kidney beans, drained
12 taco shells, warmed
1 head iceberg lettuce, shredded fine
1 or 2 ripe avocados, peeled and sliced thin
Chopped Italian parsley or fresh coriander (cilantro)

In large kettle over medium heat cook beef until crumbly, stirring to break up. Add onion and pepper. Sauté, stirring occasionally, until vegetables are tender. Stir in tomatoes, water, tomato paste, chili powder, salt, ground coriander, cumin, thyme, oregano, vinegar, chocolate, and garlic. Simmer uncovered, stirring occasionally, 1 hour 45 minutes or until thickened. Add beans; cook 15 minutes. To serve, spoon chili beef into taco shells, garnish with shredded lettuce and avocado, and sprinkle with chopped parsley or coriander.

Liederkranz with Onion on Pumpernickel Bread
MAKES 2 SANDWICHES

Although it originated in New York, Liederkranz soon traveled to the Midwest, where it is now made. A strong cheese with a robust flavor, it is at its best with dark bread and a few slices of mild onion. A good companion is cold beer or a Moselle wine.

4 ounces well-ripened Liederkranz
4 slices pumpernickel bread
1 sweet red onion, sliced thin

Spread Liederkranz on all 4 slices of bread, top 2 slices with slices of onion, and then close sandwich with remaining bread.

Denver Sandwiches
MAKES 4 SANDWICHES

Originally the filling of the Denver Sandwich was made with beaten egg combined with minced onion and bits of crisp-fried bacon. That early version is good but not as good as this one, flavored with ham and green pepper.

   Butter or margarine
   2 small onions, chopped
   1 green pepper, seeded and chopped
   ½ pound cooked smoked ham, finely diced
   8 eggs
   Salt and freshly ground black pepper to taste
   8 slices home-style white bread

In a medium-size frying pan, melt 1 tablespoon butter or margarine and add onion and green pepper. Sauté for a few minutes until onion is pale golden and add diced ham. Beat eggs, add to pan, and stir gently. Allow eggs to set and brown on one side and then turn to brown lightly on other side. Cut into 4 wedges, season with salt and pepper, and serve between slices of buttered bread or toast.

Patty Melt
MAKES 2 SANDWICHES

In California the word *melt* in the name of a sandwich means melted cheese, often Monterey Jack because it melts so smoothly. This particular "melt" is one of the most popular. There is also a Tuna Melt and a vegetarian's delight called Avocado Melt.

   ½ pound ground chuck
   ½ teaspoon salt
   ⅛ to ¼ teaspoon freshly ground black pepper
   1 teaspoon vegetable oil
   1 large onion, sliced
   4 slices rye bread
   2 slices Monterey Jack cheese
   1 tablespoon butter or margarine

Combine beef, salt, and pepper and mix lightly. Shape into 2 patties. In a greased heavy frying pan, grill hamburger patties over medium-high heat 4 to 5 minutes per side for rare and 6 minutes per side for medium. Add vegetable oil to pan and then onions. Sauté onions until soft and golden brown. Top 2 slices of bread with hamburgers, then with onions, a slice of cheese, and remaining slices of bread. Lightly butter outside of sandwich and grill on a griddle or in a heavy frying pan until brown on both sides and cheese is melted (if you prefer, you can make the sandwich with rye toast and melt the cheese under a broiler).

California Sprout, Avocado, and Cheese Sandwich
MAKES 2 SANDWICHES

Good both cold and hot. When you grill under the broiler until cheese melts, you have an Avocado Melt, but the sandwich has an especially fresh taste when it's served cold on a hot summer day.

> 4 slices Sesame Whole Wheat Bread or other substantial whole grain bread
> 2 tablespoons mayonnaise
> ½ cup alfalfa sprouts
> ½ avocado, peeled and sliced
> Salt and black pepper
> 1 medium tomato, sliced
> 2 slices Monterey Jack or white Cheddar cheese

Spread 4 slices bread with mayonnaise. Cover 2 with sprouts, top with avocado slices, season with salt and pepper, and top with tomato slices, then cheese slices, and finally remaining slices of bread.

Note: For a variation, try moistening the sprouts with a tablespoon of Yogurt Dressing.

Oregon Salmon Salad on French Rolls
MAKES 4 SANDWICHES

Cold poached salmon is one of the pleasures of summer in Oregon, and another treat is this salmon salad made from fresh poached salmon. It's a festive idea for a summer Sunday lunch. Serve white sangría or minted iced tea with it.

2 or 3 Poached Salmon Steaks, chilled (recipe below)
½ cup Blender Mayonnaise
1 teaspoon minced fresh tarragon or fresh dill
1 tablespoon finely chopped parsley
1 teaspoon lemon juice
Freshly ground black pepper to taste
4 round French rolls
3 or 6 leaves Bibb or Boston lettuce

Flake fish in a small bowl. Add mayonnaise, tarragon or dill, parsley, lemon juice, and pepper and toss to combine. Split rolls and spread salmon salad generously on roll bottoms. Top with lettuce, and close with remaining slices of bread. Or serve open-faced, putting lettuce on bread and topping each slice with a generous spoonful of salmon salad.

Poached Salmon Steaks
4 cups water
1 tablespoon white wine or white distilled vinegar
3 peppercorns
½ bay leaf
Sprig of parsley
1 teaspoon salt
2 medium salmon steaks (3 if small)

In a frying pan combine all ingredients except the salmon for the court bouillon and bring to a boil, then reduce heat and simmer for 10 to 15 minutes. Bring the court bouillon to a boil again, add the fish steaks and again reduce to a simmer. Cook for about 8 to 10 minutes, depending on the thickness of the steaks, until the fish flakes easily. Lift fish out of pan and set aside to cool. Cover and chill in refrigerator. (You may use the court bouillon as the basis of a fish soup, if you wish.)

Crab Louis on Sourdough Rolls
MAKES 2 SANDWICHES

In San Francisco, Crab Louis is usually served as a salad, but it makes a wonderful summer sandwich, too, especially when served on a mildly tangy sourdough roll.

½ pound crab meat, flaked
Louis Dressing (recipe below)
2 sourdough rolls, 6 inches long
1 cucumber, peeled and sliced
¼ head iceberg lettuce, shredded
Salt and black pepper

Combine crab meat with dressing and toss to mix thoroughly. Slice rolls in half horizontally and put a layer of cucumber slices on bottoms, then a layer of shredded lettuce, and top with crab. Add salt and pepper to taste and close with tops of rolls.

Louis Dressing
½ cup mayonnaise
1 tablespoon chili sauce
1 tablespoon chopped scallion
½ teaspoon prepared horseradish
½ teaspoon Worcestershire sauce

Combine all ingredients and stir to blend thoroughly.

5 › INTERNATIONAL SPECIALTIES

IN SOME PARTS OF THE WORLD—ESPECIALLY SCANDINAVIA—SAND-wich making has been raised to a high art, and cafés and sandwich shops abound with delectable choices. In other countries—notably France and Russia—sandwiches are reserved for hasty snacks and picnics. In the Middle East sandwiches on pita or pocket bread are sold by street vendors, but usually only one or two kinds will dominate the whole country. In Greece it is grilled skewered lamb; in Israel it is falafel; in Morocco it is chopped lamb on skewers. All along the sunny Mediterranean coast of France and Italy there are sandwiches that make superlative use of the region's abundant foods.

If you and your family have had one tuna fish salad or grilled cheese sandwich too many, the international sampling we offer here will reawaken your appetites and add a bright sense of adventure to lunches and suppers. Many of these are as easy to make as any American favorite. Others require more time and effort but are well worth it. Whenever a sandwich has become beloved of a whole people you can be sure that it has something interesting to offer. So it seems more than likely that you will find many of this collection happy additions to your sandwich repertoire.

▶ *France*

Croque Monsieur
MAKES 4 SANDWICHES

There are a number of versions of this delightful French sandwich—one very plain and buttery, one French-toasted, and another grilled and then bathed in a cheese sauce. The simplest version is considered by many to be the best because each ingredient seems to shine.

> 8 slices White Wheat Germ Bread or other firm-textured
>   white sandwich bread
> 6 to 8 tablespoons clarified butter (see note) or margarine
> 8 slices Gruyère or Monterey Jack cheese
> 4 slices boiled smoked ham
> Cornichons (French sour gherkin pickles)

Brush 4 slices of bread with butter or margarine. Top each with cheese slice, ham slice, and another cheese slice. Top each sandwich with bread that has been brushed with butter or margarine. Press the sandwiches down firmly. Remove the crusts and brush the entire outside of the sandwich with butter, including the edges. Put approximately 2 tablespoons butter in a large frying pan on a griddle and grill the sandwiches slowly over medium heat for 3 minutes. Turn and weight the sandwiches with 4 heavy saucers. Cook for an additional 3 or 4 minutes until golden brown. Serve with cornichons.

Note: To clarify butter, in a small saucepan melt butter and skim foam from top. Carefully pour the clear melted butter to another pan, leaving the milky residue in the first pan.

Pan Bagna

MAKES 4 SANDWICHES

In Nice and Cannes, on the sunny Mediterranean coast of France, these richly seasoned sandwiches are sold by street vendors and in sidewalk cafés. Some ingredients vary with the season and the sandwich maker's preference, but the indispensable elements are light crusty French bread or rolls and olive oil—and usually garlic. Also the technique of weighting the sandwich for at least half an hour is essential to combine flavors and achieve the traditional firm texture.

    4 crusty French rolls or a 28-inch loaf French bread
    4 tablespoons olive oil
    2 cloves garlic, peeled and halved
    8-ounce jar black olives, preferably Greek or Italian
    4-ounce jar pimientos, sliced or chopped
    1 small red onion, thinly sliced
    2 small tomatoes, thinly sliced
    2-ounce can flat anchovy fillets, drained, or 3-ounce can
       solid white tuna

Cut rolls or bread in half lengthwise and brush both halves with olive oil. Rub with garlic. Remove pits from olives and scatter pieces of olive over bottom half of bread. Top with pimiento, onion, tomatoes, and anchovy fillets or tuna. Cover with top of rolls or bread, place layer of waxed paper over sandwiches, and weight with a heavy plate and other heavy objects for at least 30 minutes. If loaf of French bread is used, slice into four sections after weighting.

▸ *Italy*

Cuscinetti Filanti al Prosciutto
MAKES 8 SMALL PIECES

These crusty golden "cushions" are usually served as an appetizer in Italy, but they make a delightful luncheon or supper dish, especially when served with a romaine and walnut salad and a good white wine.

2 slices mozzarella cheese
4 very thin slices prosciutto
4 slices firm-textured white bread, crusts removed
¼ cup milk
¼ cup all-purpose flour
1 egg, beaten with 1 tablespoon water
¼ cup olive oil
¾ cup vegetable oil

Make 2 sandwiches by placing mozzarella and prosciutto between slices of bread. Dip the outsides of the sandwiches in milk, then in flour, then in egg. Fry in hot oils on both sides until light brown. Cut each sandwich into 4 triangles. Serve immediately.

Neapolitan Cheese and Anchovy Toast
MAKES 8 OPEN-FACED TRIANGLES

Like the famous pizza of Naples, these oregano-scented sandwiches combine cheese, tomato, and olive oil as well as anchovies. They make a wonderful after-theater supper with a garden-fresh green salad and a bottle of robust chianti.

4 slices firm-textured white bread, crusts removed
¼ pound mozzarella or Bel Paese cheese, sliced thin
8 anchovy fillets, drained
8 thin slices tomato
Oregano
Freshly ground black pepper
3 tablespoons olive oil

Lightly toast bread. Cut each slice into 2 triangles and arrange on an oiled cookie sheet. Top each triangle with cheese cut to cover bread completely. Cut anchovies in two and make a V over each cheese triangle. Top with 1 slice tomato and sprinkle with oregano and pepper. Drizzle olive oil over each triangle. Bake in 350° F. oven for 12 to 15 minutes until cheese is melted and bread crisp.

► Greece

Fried Feta or Kasseri on Pita
MAKES 1 SANDWICH

Both these Greek cheeses are especially good when grilled or fried in olive oil or butter. Greeks often serve them with a squeeze of lemon.

1 tablespoon butter or olive oil
3 slices feta or kasseri cheese, ½ inch thick
1 loaf Pita
¼ lemon

Melt butter or oil in a small frying pan. When it bubbles, add slices of cheese and reduce heat to moderate. Fry until cheese is golden. Serve in warmed pita bread pocket with a squeeze of lemon.

Arni Souvlakia, or Grilled Lamb on Skewers

MAKES 4 SANDWICHES

In Athens, street vendors sell crusty brown grilled lamb on skewers, which they cook over braziers on their carts. Usually slices of onions and bay leaves are threaded on the skewers between the cubes of meat. To serve, the meat is pushed off the skewers into warm pita bread.

1½ pounds boneless leg or lean shoulder of lamb
½ teaspoon oregano or imported Greek wild marjoram
4 tablespoons olive oil
2 tablespoons lemon juice
½ teaspoon salt
Freshly ground black pepper
3 onions, quartered
4 bay leaves, cut in half
4 loaves Pita

Cut lamb into ¾-inch cubes and combine in bowl with oregano or marjoram, olive oil, lemon juice, salt, and pepper. Marinate for at least 2 hours, preferably longer. When ready to cook, thread the meat on skewers, adding pieces of onion and bay leaf between each 2 cubes of meat. Grill over charcoal or under broiler for 7 to 10 minutes per side, until outside is brown and inside is still slightly pink. Meanwhile warm pita in 350° F. oven for about 5 minutes. Fill pita pockets with hot lamb.

▸ Israel

Falafel in Pita
MAKES 8 SANDWICHES

These spicy chickpea patties are so popular in Israel that they can be bought from street vendors or in cafés all day long. A slightly different version, made from fava beans, is the national dish of Egypt. As a snack falafel are served in pita bread with chopped tomatoes and shredded lettuce or chopped cucumbers as well as a delicious tahini dressing. A falafel (the accent is on the second syllable) mix is now available in Middle Eastern specialty stores, but the real thing is tastier.

> 1 pound dried chickpeas, soaked in water to cover for 24 hours
> 2 onions, finely chopped
> 4 scallions, chopped
> 2 cloves garlic, peeled and crushed or pressed
> 3 tablespoons finely chopped parsley
> 1 teaspoon cumin
> ¼ teaspoon ground red pepper
> 1 teaspoon salt
> ½ teaspoon baking powder
> ¼ cup all-purpose flour
> Vegetable oil for frying
> 8 loaves Pita, warmed
> Tomato and Lettuce Salad (recipe below)
> Tahini Dressing (recipe below)

Drain the chickpeas and grind to a meal or pulp in a meat grinder or processor. In a bowl mix chickpea pulp, onions, scallions, garlic, parsley, cumin, red pepper, salt, baking powder, and flour and stir to combine thoroughly. Put mixture through grinder or processor again. Let rest for 15 minutes and then form into balls about 1 inch in diameter. Let rest for 15 minutes and then deep-fry in hot oil for 5 minutes in batches, turning falafel to brown all over. Drain on paper towels. Serve in warmed pita with a tablespoon each of Tomato and Lettuce Salad and Tahini Dressing.

Tomato and Lettuce Salad

2 medium tomatoes, chopped
½ head iceberg lettuce, finely shredded and chopped

Combine tomatoes and lettuce.

Tahini Dressing

1 cup tahini (sesame paste)
1 clove garlic, crushed or pressed
1 teaspoon salt
½ cup lemon juice
½ cup water, or more to achieve a thick creamy consistency

In a blender combine all ingredients and blend to combine thoroughly. You may do this by hand, but a blender makes a smoother sauce.

▶ Middle East

Armenian Khemya Kebab
MAKES 6 SANDWICHES

Grilled ground lamb or beef on skewers is popular throughout the Middle East. Seasonings vary from country to country, even from town to town, but the succulent, richly spiced "sausages" are always a flavorful treat.

2 pounds ground lamb, finely chopped
2 small onions, finely chopped
3 tablespoons finely chopped parsley
2 teaspoons salt
¼ teaspoon cumin
1 teaspoon paprika
¼ teaspoon black pepper
1 onion, thinly sliced
½ cup chopped parsley
1 teaspoon paprika
6 loaves Pita, warmed

In a bowl combine the first seven ingredients and stir with fork or blend with hands to mix thoroughly. Shape into balls 1 inch in diameter and push them on skewers, shaping each ball into a "sausage" around the skewer. Broil the kebabs over charcoal or under a broiler, grilling 7 minutes and then turning to grill other side for 5 to 7 minutes. In a small bowl, combine the sliced onion, ½ cup parsley, and paprika for the garnish. Serve cooked kebabs in warm pita bread pockets with a sprinkling of garnish.

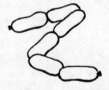

▸ Switzerland

Bratwurst on a Crusty Roll
MAKES 4 SANDWICHES

In Zurich these fine-textured fresh veal sausages (sometimes pork and beef may be added) are broiled or sautéed until brown and crisp and served on large hard rolls with Düsseldorf mustard.

1 tablespoon vegetable oil
1 tablespoon butter or margarine
4 large or 8 small bratwurst
Four 6-inch hard rolls, French or sourdough
Düsseldorf or other German mustard

In a large frying pan heat oil and melt butter or margarine until bubbling stops. Add bratwurst and cook over medium heat until golden brown on all sides, 18 to 20 minutes. Heat rolls for 5 minutes in 350° F. oven, then cut in half lengthwise. Spread bottom of each roll with mustard, add a bratwurst, or 2 if they are small, then close with top of roll.

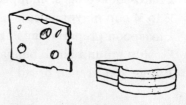

Swiss Roasted Cheese Sandwich
MAKES 6 SANDWICHES

At first thought, this may seem almost like a breakfast dish—and it does make a lovely winter brunch—but it is served in Swiss restaurants for lunch and snacks.

6 slices firm-textured white bread
1 cup half-and-half
Six 1-ounce slices Swiss cheese
About 1 tablespoon caraway seeds

Dip bread slices in half-and-half. Place on a buttered cookie sheet and top each slice with cheese. Sprinkle caraway seeds over each. Bake in 400° F. oven for 7 to 10 minutes, until cheese is melted and bread very hot.

Gefülltes Brot
SERVES 6 TO 8

A savory stuffed French loaf is a popular snack among the Swiss. In this recipe we use ground cooked ham as the main ingredient, but you could use rare beef, roast veal, ground cooked chicken, or chicken livers. Ideal for picnics.

    2 cups ground cooked smoked ham
    1 sour pickle, finely chopped
    3 tablespoons grated onion
    2 tablespoons minced parsley
    2 hard-cooked eggs, chopped
    ½ to ¾ cup mayonnaise
    1 teaspoon prepared mustard
    Freshly ground black pepper
    1 large loaf French bread

In a bowl combine ham, pickle, onion, parsley, eggs, mayonnaise (enough to bind), and mustard, and stir to blend thoroughly. Add pepper to taste. Cut off the ends of the loaf of bread and remove the doughy inside with a knife or fork. The bread case should be about ¾ inch thick. Cover one end with aluminum foil and stuff the meat stuffing into the other end, making sure to press it firmly. Wrap the whole loaf in foil and chill in the refrigerator for several hours before cutting in 2-inch slices to serve.

▶ Germany

Knockwurst
MAKES 2 SANDWICHES

Like their Italian neighbors, the Germans win top honors for imaginative sausage making. In fact, in Bavaria alone one can buy more than twenty-five different kinds of sausages. Often a varied sampling of these *wursts* is served on a plate with mounds of tangy sauerkraut and potato pancakes. However, many cafés and beer gardens also sell sausages as snacks or quick lunches, and these are frequently wrapped in a slice of crusty white bread and topped with mustard or tomato sauce.

> 2 or 4 large slices Italian or sourdough bread
> 2 knockwurst
> Düsseldorf or other German mustard

In a saucepan bring to a boil enough water to cover knockwurst, add the sausages, and simmer for 5 to 8 minutes, until heated through. If bread slices are not large enough to wrap around a whole sausage, cut knockwurst in half lengthwise and serve on 2 slices of bread. Top with mustard.

Westphalian Ham on a Crusty Roll
MAKES 2 SANDWICHES

In Munich as well as in other German cities people often have two breakfasts (or one light breakfast and one brunch at eleven o'clock). The second breakfast may be cold cuts and bread or hot sausage or—one of the simplest and best—Westphalian ham on a Kaiser Semmel, which is a large crusty roll. You can make semmels yourself from the recipe for Crusty Italian Bread, using the baking time for small loaves and shaping the rolls in small round shapes about 4 inches across.

> 2 crusty round rolls
> Butter
> ¼ pound Westphalian ham or prosciutto
> Düsseldorf or other German mustard

Slice tops from rolls. Butter bottoms of rolls and place ham to cover entire roll. Spread mustard on cut side of top and cover ham.

▶ Latin America

Peruvian Buttifarras
MAKES 8 SANDWICHES

These hearty sandwiches feature a rich pot roasted or braised pork shoulder served on crusty rolls. Lightly pickled onions add a tangy note.

> 2 to 3 cloves garlic, crushed or pressed
> ½ teaspoon cumin
> 1 teaspoon salt
> 1 scant teaspoon black pepper
> 3-pound pork shoulder, boned and rolled
> 8 crusty rolls
> Pickled Onions (recipe below)

Mash garlic and combine with cumin, salt, and pepper. Rub meat with garlic mixture. Let stand for 1 to 2 hours. Heat oven to 425° F. Put roast in casserole dish and add enough water to almost cover. Roast for about 45 minutes. Reduce heat to 325° F., cover, and roast for about 1½ hours, until meat is cooked. Remove meat from casserole, cool slightly, and slice. Serve on rolls with a topping of Pickled Onions.

Pickled Onions (*Escabeche de Cebolla*)
> 2 red onions, thinly sliced
> ¼ teaspoon oregano
> 1 hot pepper, thinly sliced (optional)
> ¼ teaspoon salt
> Freshly ground black pepper (if hot pepper is not used)
> ½ cup white vinegar, mixed with ¼ cup water

Combine all ingredients and refrigerate overnight. Drain onions before using on sandwiches.

Cuban Sandwiches
MAKES 2 SANDWICHES

In one of those magical transformations that abound in sandwich making, the simple ingredients of this sandwich combine to create an unforgettable treat. In the United States, wherever there are expatriate Cubans there are shops selling these succulent sandwiches.

The secret to this sandwich is that the roast pork should be home-cooked loin that has been rubbed with garlic before roasting. The rolled pork roast sold in delicatessens will not be moist or rich enough in taste.

1 loaf crisp light French bread
Butter or margarine
¼ pound sliced cooked smoked ham
¼ pound sliced Swiss cheese
6 slices roast pork loin
Dijon mustard
Sour pickles

Cut loaf of bread in half lengthwise and butter bottom half. Cover with ham slices, then cheese, then pork slices. Spread top with mustard and cover sandwich. Press top down firmly and cut in half. Cuban sandwiches are sometimes heated to crisp the bread and blend the flavors. To heat, place in a 300° F. oven for 5 to 7 minutes. Serve with sour pickles as garnish.

▸ *Scandinavia*

DANISH SMØRREBRØD, OR
OPEN-FACED SANDWICHES

All the Scandinavians love open-faced sandwiches, but the Danes are the acknowledged geniuses when it comes to imaginative and delectable combinations. In Copenhagen there are restaurants that feature over a hundred different kinds. Many of these have now become classics, and we offer recipes for several of the most familiar. But don't hesitate to create your own variations on the theme, because one of the great pleasures of this style of sandwich making is creating just the right combination of good things to suit your taste. Each of the following recipes is for one sandwich.

Rush-Hour Shrimp

1 tablespoon whipped butter
1 slice firm-textured white bread
20 or more very small boiled shrimp
Thin slice of lemon, cut in quarters
Sprig of fresh dill

Butter the bread and arrange the shrimp in a symmetrical layer. Top with lemon and decorate with dill.

Smoked Salmon

1 tablespoon whipped butter
1 slice Danish rye bread
2 or 3 thin slices smoked salmon
1 thin slice raw onion, separated into rings
Sprig of fresh dill or sliced cucumber pickle

Butter the bread and arrange smoked salmon neatly on it. Garnish with onion rings and dill sprig or a few slices of pickled cucumber.

Pickled Herring

1 tablespoon whipped butter
1 slice Sour Rye Bread
3 to 4 slices pickled herring
4 to 5 thin rings raw onion
2 to 3 strips pimiento

Butter bread and arrange herring neatly on top. Garnish with onion and pimiento.

Smoked Tongue

1 slice Sour Rye Bread
1 tablespoon Horseradish Butter
1 leaf lettuce, preferably Bibb
2 to 3 thin slices smoked tongue
1 hard-cooked egg, sliced
½ teaspoon chopped chives

Spread bread with Horseradish Butter, top with lettuce leaf, then with smoked tongue, then with 3 slices hard-cooked egg. Garnish with chives.

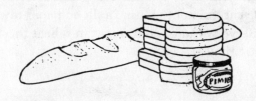

Roast Beef

1 tablespoon whipped butter
1 slice Sour Rye Bread
1 thin slice roast beef
Thin slices of onion
Cucumber pickle slice

Butter bread and arrange beef neatly on it. Arrange onion over it and top with pickle.

Danish Blue Cheese

1 tablespoon whipped butter
1 slice Sour Rye Bread
2 to 3 thin slices Danish blue cheese
3 thin slices tomato
1 to 2 tablespoons Danish Fried Onions (recipe below)

Butter bread and top with blue cheese. Top with tomato slices and garnish with onions.

Danish Fried Onions
2 medium onions
Oil for deep frying
Salt

Peel and slice onions very thin. Heat oil to 375° F. and cook onions, one onion at a time, for 5 minutes until crisp and brown. Be careful not to burn. Drain on paper towels, then salt to taste. Serve warm or cold. You can reheat these in a 350° F. oven for 5 minutes.

FINNISH OPEN-FACED SANDWICHES
Like the Danes, the Finns are extremely fond of open-faced sandwiches. The Finns, too, have traditional combinations that are offered at cafés, train stations, and even on excursion boats that ply the Baltic and the innumerable lakes of Finland. Here are some favorites. Each recipe is for one sandwich.

Anchovy and Sliced Egg

1 tablespoon whipped butter
1 slice dark rye bread
1 leaf Boston lettuce
1 hard-cooked egg, sliced
2 or 3 anchovy fillets, drained
Sprig of fresh dill

Butter the bread and top with lettuce, then egg slices. Arrange anchovies crisscrossed on top. Place dill sprig in center.

Finnish Herring. This is made just exactly the same as the Anchovy and Sliced Egg above, but 2 small herring fillets are crisscrossed on top of the sandwich in place of the anchovies.

Roast Pork

1 tablespoon whipped butter
1 slice dark rye bread
2 thin slices roast pork
2 to 3 slices pickled beets, cut in strips
4 thin slices dill pickle

Butter bread and arrange pork neatly on top. Center beets and place pickles in corners of bread.

6· SANDWICH PARTIES FOR YEAR-ROUND ENTERTAINING

SANDWICHES AND INFORMAL ENTERTAINING SEEM TO GO TOGETHER. Having neighbors and other friends over for a convivial backyard hamburger barbecue is now a tradition all across the United States. Not to be left out, city dwellers have developed such sandwich party ideas as make-your-own-hero and fill-your-own-taco as well as a variety of sandwich brunches and soup and sandwich suppers. Yet even though it's generally true that sandwich parties tend to be casual and easygoing, if you have ever attended a formal tea or a gala midnight supper that featured a selection of pâtés, exotic cheeses, and crusty French bread, you know that the possibilities for entertaining with sandwiches are almost limitless. They range from a simple lunch-hour picnic in a city park to a festive holiday brunch, from a Scandinavian breakfast-buffet to a Middle Eastern pita party, from a spontaneous what-can-we-feed-the-gang gathering to a carefully planned steak sandwich party with Oriental overtones. The scope is enormous, and the menus we offer here are only a beginning.

140

All of our parties are planned around seasonal foods that are affordable, and we've made sure that do-ahead recipes predominate and easy service is a significant feature. To make the whole process even easier we suggest the party planner's standby—a written master plan. If you write it all down, things will go much more smoothly. And we believe in putting *everything* on the list: a timetable; food and drink supplies; household supplies such as napkins, glasses, candles; and most important of all, a list of congenial people. Because these are such easy parties to give and to enjoy, they offer a wonderful opportunity to introduce new acquaintances to old friends in a relaxed social atmosphere.

The recipes are designed to serve eight, but many can be expanded with a little care. However, recipes for drinks and for breads, cakes, and baked desserts should simply be made a second or third time if you plan to serve more than eight.

The best thing we can say about sandwich parties is that everybody loves them—hosts and guests alike. They seem to suit our way of life.

▶ Festive Spring or Easter Brunch

You can serve this same menu at other times of the year, but it is most appropriate for a spring day because it uses the first strawberries and the first asparagus of the season.

  * Sliced Strawberries and Grapefruit Sections in Orange Juice
  * Ham and Asparagus on Muffins with Cheese Sauce
  * Cinnamon-Nut Biscuits
    Coffee and Tea

Sliced Strawberries and Grapefruit Sections in Orange Juice
SERVES 8

4 large smooth-skinned white grapefruit
3 pints strawberries, washed, hulled, and halved
1 cup orange juice

With a sharp paring knife peel the grapefruit over a bowl to catch juice, then cut out sections between white membranes. Combine grapefruit sections, strawberries, and orange juice in a bowl and toss lightly to mix.

Ham and Asparagus on Muffins with Cheese Sauce
SERVES 8

32 asparagus spears
1½ tablespoons butter or margarine
8 large or 16 small thin slices cooked ham
8 English muffins
Cheese Sauce (recipe below)
Finely chopped chives or parsley

Trim asparagus, removing white tough portions. Wash in cold running water. Simmer asparagus in lightly salted water until crisp-tender, from 5 to 10 minutes depending on size. Melt butter or margarine in a large frying pan and quickly sauté ham slices on both sides until lightly brown and heated through. Split muffins with a fork and toast under broiler. Assemble sandwiches by covering each muffin half with ½ large slice or 1 small slice sautéed ham, 2 asparagus spears, and Cheese Sauce. Sprinkle with chives or parsley and serve at once.

Cheese Sauce
3 tablespoons butter or margarine
4 tablespoons all-purpose flour
2½ cups milk, heated to just below boiling
½ cup grated Gruyère or white Cheddar cheese
½ teaspoon salt
Freshly ground black pepper

In a medium-size heavy-bottomed skillet melt butter or margarine and stir in flour, 1 tablespoon at a time. Cook over moderate heat 2 minutes or so, stirring constantly. Remove pan from heat and add milk, ½ cup at a time, stirring with wire whisk until thoroughly blended. Return to heat and stir until sauce thickens. Simmer, stirring, for about 5 minutes. Add cheese and stir until it melts. Season with salt and pepper and stir again.

Cinnamon-Nut Biscuits
MAKES 12 BISCUITS

Quick to make and delightful to eat, these mildly sweet biscuits add the perfect finishing touch to a springtime brunch.

¼ cup sugar
¼ cup chopped walnuts or pecans
½ teaspoon cinnamon
2 cups buttermilk biscuit mix
½ cup cold water
3 tablespoons butter or margarine, melted

Mix sugar, nuts, and cinnamon and set aside. Prepare mix according to package directions, using the cold water. Shape in ball and put on lightly floured waxed paper. Press down slightly, then cut in 12 equal pieces. Shape each in ball; roll in melted butter or margarine, then in nut mixture. Arrange in 8-

inch round layer cake pan, pressing down slightly. Bake in preheated 400° F. oven for 15 minutes, or until lightly browned and done. Serve warm.

▶ Summer Sandwich Brunch

Fresh Orange Juice or Mimosas (champagne and orange juice over crushed ice)
* French-Toasted Canadian Bacon and Cheese Sandwiches
* Whole Wheat Nut Quick Bread and Honey Walnut Butter
* Cantaloupe-Blueberry Fruit Cup with Sour Cream
Coffee or Tea

French-Toasted Canadian Bacon and Cheese Sandwiches
MAKES 8 SANDWICHES

16 slices Canadian bacon
16 slices cracked wheat or White Wheat Germ Bread
Dijon mustard
8 slices (1 ounce) Monterey Jack cheese
Butter or margarine
2 eggs
½ cup milk

Sauté bacon for 5 minutes in nonstick pan, turning once. Spread 8 slices of bread with mustard. Cover with bacon slices, then with cheese. Lightly spread remaining slices of bread with butter or margarine and use to close sandwiches. In a pie plate or shallow bowl, beat together eggs and milk. Dip both sides of sandwich in egg mixture. Grill on hot well-buttered griddle or frying pan over medium heat until golden brown on both sides. Serve at once or keep warm in very low oven for 10 minutes or so if necessary.

Whole Wheat Nut Quick Bread and Honey Walnut Butter

MAKES 1 LOAF

Make this spicy nut bread the day before your party so that it will slice well for sandwiches. This simple combination of familiar ingredients is so good you may want to make two loaves.

1 cup all-purpose flour
½ cup whole wheat flour
2 teaspoons baking powder
½ teaspoon cinnamon
½ teaspoon ground ginger
¼ teaspoon salt
¼ cup (½ stick) butter or margarine, softened
¾ cup sugar
2 eggs
⅔ cup milk
½ teaspoon vanilla extract
½ cup chopped walnuts
Honey Walnut Butter (recipe below)

In a medium-size mixing bowl combine both flours, baking powder, cinnamon, ginger, and salt. Stir to combine thoroughly. In another bowl cream together butter or margarine and sugar until fluffy; add eggs, one at a time, beating after each until mixture is smooth. Then alternately add flour mixture and milk to egg mixture. Add vanilla. Stir until mixture is smooth. Stir in walnuts. Pour batter into greased 8-by-4-by-3-inch loaf pan. Bake in preheated 350° F. oven for 1 hour. Remove from oven and leave loaf in pan to cool for 10 minutes. Remove gently from pan and cool thoroughly on cake rack before slicing. Slice loaf into sixteen ½-inch slices and spread 8 slices with Honey Walnut Butter. Top with remaining 8 slices and cut in half.

Honey Walnut Butter

½ cup (1 stick) butter or margarine, softened
¼ cup honey
¼ cup finely chopped toasted walnuts

Beat butter or margarine with fork until fluffy. Gradually beat in honey and toasted walnuts. (To toast walnuts, spread a layer of nuts on cake pan and toast in 350° F. oven before chopping.) Store butter in refrigerator until shortly before serving. Soften slightly at room temperature before spreading.

Cantaloupe-Blueberry Fruit Cup with Sour Cream
SERVES 8

3 medium-size ripe cantaloupes, peeled, seeded, and cubed
1 pint blueberries, washed and drained
1 cup orange juice
1 pint sour cream
3 tablespoons grated orange rind

In a glass bowl combine cantaloupe cubes and blueberries. Pour orange juice over fruit and toss gently with two spoons to mix thoroughly. Spoon into sherbet glasses or dessert dishes and top with a spoonful of sour cream and a sprinkling of grated orange rind.

▸ Scandinavian Winter Breakfast-Brunch

In Finland as well as in the other Scandinavian countries where winter sports are generally a way of life, cold-weather breakfasts can be quite imposing. In the big hotels in Helsinki, for example, the breakfast buffet very nearly rivals the evening smorgasbord. There is sliced ham, beef salami, Baltic herring, the superlative Finnish Swiss cheese, flavored and unflavored yogurt, eggs, and a dazzling array of light and dark breads and rolls, plus sweet butter, jams, and good strong coffee. Except for the yogurt, all of these foods lend themselves to sandwich making, and such hearty fare is the perfect prelude to your own ice skating or cross-country skiing party.

Choose your own favorites from the following:

Assorted Breads, including Scandinavian Rye, Finnish-Style Health Bread, Seeded Whole Wheat Sandwich Buns, Sour Rye, Crusty White Rolls, Rye Flatbreads
Cheeses: Swiss, Edam, Crema Dania, Havarti
Sliced Cold Meats: Boiled Ham, Beef Salami, Thuringer, Sliced Tongue
Eggs: 8-minute eggs (halfway between soft and hard-cooked)
Creamed Herring
Sweet Butter
Jams: Strawberry, Raspberry, Lingonberry
Yogurt: Flavored and Plain
Coffee

▸ Come-Watch-the-Game Hot Dog Party

* Fresh Raw Vegetables with Two-Cheese Dip
  Sesame Breadsticks
* Hot Dogs with All the Trimmings
* Spicy Chickpea Salad
* Pineapple-Orange Boats
* Melt-in-the-Mouth Almond Cookies
  Beer, Iced Tea, Lemonade

Fresh Raw Vegetables with Two-Cheese Dip

Carrot sticks
Celery sticks
Broccoli florets
Cauliflower florets
Small raw green beans
Cucumber spears
Radishes
Two-Cheese Dip (recipe below)

Two-Cheese Dip

MAKES ABOUT 3½ CUPS

Two 8-ounce containers creamed cottage cheese
4 ounces blue cheese
½ cup half-and-half
2 tablespoons sliced scallions
2 tablespoons finely minced parsley
Paprika

Put cheeses and half-and-half in blender and whirl a few seconds until smooth. Do not overblend. Pour into a bowl, add scallions and parsley, and stir to blend well. Sprinkle with paprika.

Hot Dogs with All the Trimmings

16 to 20 frankfurters (2 pounds)
16 to 20 frankfurter rolls, heated
Selection of mustards
Sauerkraut (recipe below)
Paprika Onions (recipe below)
Chili (recipe below)
Chopped raw onions

Place frankfurters in saucepan with small amount of boiling water, reduce heat, cover, and simmer for 5 minutes or until heated through. Do not boil. Place frankfurters in heated rolls and serve with choice of toppings.

Sauerkraut
1 pound sauerkraut
1 cup water
1 teaspoon caraway seeds

Drain sauerkraut and rinse under cold water. Place in saucepan and add water and caraway seeds. Bring to a boil, reduce heat, cover, and simmer until heated through.

Paprika Onions
6 medium onions
3 tablespoons vegetable oil
1 tablespoon paprika
½ teaspoon salt
Freshly ground black pepper to taste

Peel onions and cut in half. Slice into thin slices. Heat oil in medium frying pan, add onions, and cook over low heat until soft but not brown. Add paprika, salt, and pepper and stir to blend thoroughly. Simmer a few minutes more.

Chili
1 tablespoon vegetable oil
1 pound lean ground beef
½ cup chopped onions
1 small clove garlic, pressed
8-ounce can tomato sauce
1 to 2 teaspoons chili powder, or to taste
½ teaspoon salt
½ cup water

Heat oil in medium frying pan. Add beef and brown over medium heat. Add onions and garlic and sauté quickly. Add tomato sauce, chili powder, and salt. Add water, cover, and simmer 15 minutes.

Spicy Chickpea Salad
SERVES 8

Two 20-ounce cans chickpeas, drained (4 cups)
1 medium green pepper, slivered
2 small red onions, sliced thin and separated into rings
¼ teaspoon hot pepper sauce, or to taste
½ cup olive oil
6 tablespoons red wine vinegar
2 tablespoons capers
½ teaspoon salt, or to taste

Rinse chickpeas and drain well. In large bowl toss to mix all ingredients. Chill several hours or overnight.

Pineapple-Orange Boats
SERVES 8

2 medium pineapples
½ cup fresh orange juice
Fresh mint (optional)

With a sharp knife cut pineapple in half lengthwise. Cut each half in half lengthwise. Remove meat in one piece; then remove core. Return meat to shell and cut into slices. Drizzle each quarter with orange juice and garnish with mint sprigs if you like. Cover with plastic wrap and refrigerate until just before serving.

Melt-in-the-Mouth Almond Cookies
MAKES 50 TO 60 COOKIES

½ cup butter, softened
1 cup packed light brown sugar
1 teaspoon vanilla extract
1 egg
¾ cup all-purpose flour
1 teaspoon double-acting baking powder
½ teaspoon salt
½ cup blanched almonds, finely chopped

Preheat the oven to 400° F. Cream the butter. Add the sugar, vanilla, and egg and beat until light. Mix together the flour, baking powder, and salt. Add to the butter mixture and mix thoroughly, then stir in the nuts. Drop by level teaspoonfuls onto ungreased cookie sheets. Bake 5 minutes. Remove from the oven and let sit exactly 1 minute, then, with a broad spatula, pressing down firmly, quickly remove from cookie sheet. Cool on wire racks. Store in airtight containers.

▸ Tea for a Sunday Afternoon

This light but satisfying tea in the British style just suits a small gathering on a brisk fall afternoon. Invite your guests to join you for a pre-tea trip to a museum, an early movie, or an invigorating walk to a nearby park. With just a bit of planning you can easily prepare most of the menu in advance. Make the seed cake the day before, the scones the morning of the party, and the sandwiches shortly before you leave for your jaunt. When you return all you will have to do is set the kettle to boiling, warm the scones in the oven, and put out sandwiches and cakes.

*Cucumber Tea Sandwiches
*Cream Cheese, Blue Cheese, and Watercress Tea Sand-
wiches
*Ham Tea Sandwiches with Scallion-Mustard Butter
*Currant Scones
Raspberry Jam
Whipped Butter or Margarine
*Seed Cake
Darjeeling, Oolong, or Other Fine Tea
Milk
Sugar Lumps

Cucumber Tea Sandwiches
MAKES 16 SMALL SANDWICHES

Whoever invented these small, elegant sandwiches deserves
our heartfelt gratitude. They are the perfect accompaniment to
a well-brewed cup of tea.

8 thin slices white bread
¼ cup whipped sweet butter, softened
1 cucumber, peeled, scored with a fork, and thinly sliced
Salt and freshly ground black pepper to taste

Remove crusts from bread and spread lightly with butter. Arrange cucumber on 4 slices, sprinkle with salt and pepper, and
top with remaining bread. To store, wrap in plastic wrap and
refrigerate until just before serving. To serve, cut each sandwich into 4 small squares or 4 narrow strips.

Cream Cheese, Blue Cheese, and Watercress Tea Sandwiches
MAKES 16 SMALL SANDWICHES

½ bunch watercress
3-ounce package cream cheese, softened
⅛ pound blue cheese
8 thin slices whole wheat bread

Wash and dry watercress, removing any tough stems. In a small bowl combine cheeses and stir to blend thoroughly. Cut crusts from bread and spread 4 slices with cheese mixture. Top cheese with 3 or 4 sprigs watercress, then top with remaining bread. Store wrapped in plastic wrap until just before serving. To serve, cut each into 4 triangles.

Ham Tea Sandwiches with Scallion-Mustard Butter
MAKES 16 SMALL SANDWICHES

These add just the right spicy note to the party menu.

8 thin slices white bread
¼ cup Scallion-Mustard Butter, softened
8 thin slices cooked ham, or 4 if large (folded for double layer)

Remove crusts from bread and spread lightly with Scallion-Mustard Butter. Top buttered bread with ham and then with remaining bread. Store covered with plastic wrap in refrigerator until just before serving. Cut each into 4 small squares or 4 narrow strips.

Currant Scones

MAKES 16 PIECES

2 cups all-purpose flour
1½ teaspoons cream of tartar
¾ teaspoon baking soda
1 teaspoon salt
½ cup butter or margarine
½ cup dried currants
1 egg
About ¾ cup buttermilk
1 egg yolk
1 tablespoon water

Sift flour, cream of tartar, baking soda, and salt into a bowl. Cut in butter or margarine with a pastry blender or two knives until mixture resembles fine bread crumbs. Add currants, whole egg, and enough buttermilk to make soft dough. Mix with a fork and turn out onto a well-floured board. Knead a few times, divide into two parts, shape into balls, and then roll out with a rolling pin to form two circles about ½ inch thick. Cut each round into eight wedge-shaped pieces like a pie. Place wedges on a greased cookie sheet with some space between each. Combine egg yolk with water and brush each scone with it. Bake in a preheated 425° F. oven for 15 minutes or until golden brown.

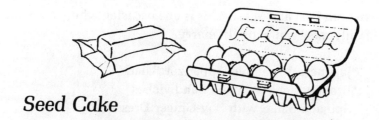

Seed Cake

A velvety pound cake that is flecked with caraway seeds, this is a traditional British tea favorite.

1 cup (2 sticks) sweet butter
1 cup sugar
5 eggs
1 teaspoon vanilla extract
2 cups all-purpose flour, sifted
1 teaspoon baking powder
½ teaspoon salt
1 tablespoon caraway seeds

In a mixing bowl cream together the butter and sugar until light and fluffy. Add the eggs, one at a time, beating thoroughly after each addition. Add the vanilla and stir well. Sift the flour with the baking powder and salt. Add flour mixture gradually to egg mixture, folding it in with a rubber spatula. Fold in the caraway seeds. Pour the batter into a greased 9-inch tube pan and bake in preheated 350° F. oven for 45 minutes or until cake tests done with a tester.

▸ Steak Teriyaki Sandwich Party

Borrowing from the many-splendored flavors of Japan, we've created an unusually delicious menu for a steak sandwich party. Although our recipes were inspired by Japanese cuisine, they are not orthodox Japanese recipes, but combine ideas from both East and West. This is one occasion where the twain not only meet but actually marry.

*Japanese Vegetable Appetizer Salad
*Broiled Steak Teriyaki Sandwiches
*Spinach Salad with Soy-Ginger Dressing
*Melon Rings or *Ginger Ice Cream
*Crisp Sesame Seed Cookies
Beer (preferably Japanese) or Green Tea

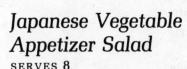

Japanese Vegetable Appetizer Salad
SERVES 8

This is a variation on a sunomono salad (which is usually vinegared cucumbers or carrots or daikon, the big white Oriental radish). Small portions of sunomono are often served with warm sake before a meal.

4 medium cucumbers
4 small carrots
1 bunch radishes
¼ cup rice wine vinegar
1 tablespoon soy sauce
1 teaspoon sugar
¼ teaspoon Oriental sesame oil

Wash cucumbers and scrub well if waxed, but do not peel. Slice into very thin slices. Wash and scrape carrots; shred finely. Thinly slice radishes. Combine all vegetables in a glass bowl. Combine vinegar, soy sauce, sugar, and sesame oil in a small bowl and mix thoroughly. Pour over vegetables.

Broiled Steak Teriyaki Sandwiches
MAKES 8 SANDWICHES

3 to 4 pounds top round beef steak (first cut)
1 cup soy sauce
¼ cup honey
1 clove garlic, finely minced or pressed
1 tablespoon rice wine vinegar
1 tablespoon freshly grated ginger
¼ tablespoon Oriental sesame oil
Eight 8-inch sourdough rolls
8 leaves Chinese cabbage, shredded

Place steak in a shallow glass or ceramic dish or in a plastic bag large enough to hold it. Combine soy sauce, honey, garlic, vinegar, ginger, and oil and blend well. Pour over meat. Cover dish (or close plastic bag with a wire twist) and marinate in refrigerator 3 to 4 hours, turning several times.

Remove steak from marinade and broil or barbecue to desired doneness. Slit rolls and toast lightly in broiler or oven. Slice steak. Cover bottom of each roll generously with slices of steak and add a light sprinkling of shredded cabbage. Ladle a tablespoon or so of meat juices (or marinade, heated) over the sandwich, top with roll half, and cut in two.

Spinach Salad with Soy-Ginger Dressing
SERVES 8

1 pound fresh spinach
8-ounce can water chestnuts, drained and sliced thin
1 tablespoon sesame seeds
Soy-Ginger Dressing (recipe below)

Rinse spinach well. Tear leaves from stems, discarding stems. Drain leaves and dry on paper towels. Place spinach and water chestnuts in a salad bowl. Place sesame seeds in a heavy-bottomed frying pan over medium heat, shaking occasionally, until seeds turn light brown. Pour dressing over spinach, sprinkle with sesame seeds, and toss lightly.

Soy-Ginger Dressing

MAKES ½ CUP

3 tablespoons water
2 tablespoons cider vinegar
2 tablespoons soy sauce
1 tablespoon peanut oil
1 teaspoon Oriental sesame oil or peanut oil
½ teaspoon sugar
⅛ to ¼ teaspoon ground ginger, to taste
1 small clove garlic, crushed

Place all ingredients in jar with tight-fitting lid and shake to mix.

Melon Rings

Cut 1 large ripe honeydew or 2 medium ripe cantaloupes into ¾-inch-thick crosswise rings. Peel and remove seeds. You may fill the center with 3 or 4 hulled strawberries or a few white grapes, halved. Sprinkle rings with fresh orange juice.

Ginger Ice Cream

SERVES 8

1 quart good-quality vanilla ice cream, softened
⅓ cup preserved ginger
2 tablespoons syrup from preserved ginger
8 teaspoons finely chopped crystallized ginger (optional)

Combine ice cream, ginger, and ginger syrup and stir to blend thoroughly. Refreeze until ready to serve. If desired sprinkle 1 teaspoon crystallized ginger over each portion.

Crisp Sesame Seed Cookies
MAKES ABOUT 2½ DOZEN COOKIES

These aren't really Japanese, but they are delicious and go well with the ginger ice cream.

½ cup butter or margarine, softened
¾ cup sugar
1 egg
1 teaspoon vanilla extract
1⅓ cups all-purpose flour
1½ teaspoons baking powder
⅛ teaspoon salt
3 tablespoons sesame seeds

Preheat oven to 375° F. In a medium bowl cream together the butter or margarine and sugar. Add egg and vanilla and beat well. Add dry ingredients except sesame seeds and stir to mix well. Roll into balls the size of small walnuts and dip tops into sesame seeds. Flatten cookies slightly between palms and place 2 inches apart on cookie sheets. Bake in preheated oven 8 to 10 minutes. Remove to racks to cool.

▸Mexican Burrito Party

Mexican cooking at its best offers a rich variety of tastes and textures that excite the interest of food lovers everywhere. For this party our menu has been planned to highlight the interesting contrasts to be found in almost every Mexican meal. The buttery coolness of Guacamole is a perfect counterbalance to tangy Salsa Cruda and the spicy Burritos are ideally complemented by the tart fresh-tasting Sangría and Licuada de Piña. While this is not a quick-to-cook menu, it is so good that it is worth the extra effort. And many of the dishes can be prepared well ahead of time.

*Guacamole
*Salsa Cruda
 Tortilla Chips
*Chicken Burritos
*Refried Bean Burritos
*Caramel Flan
*Sangría or *Licuado de Piña

Guacamole
MAKES 3 CUPS

Serve this avocado dip with tortilla chips, but reserve about half for Burritos.

2 large, very ripe avocados
1 small tomato, chopped
1 tablespoon grated onion
1 small clove garlic, crushed
1 canned green chili, chopped
2 teaspoons lemon juice
Salt and black pepper to taste
Paprika

Peel avocados and remove the pits. In a small bowl mash pulp with a fork. Add tomato, onion, garlic, green chili, and lemon juice, stirring well after each addition. Season with salt and pepper. Sprinkle with paprika. Cover well with plastic wrap and chill.

Salsa Cruda

MAKES ABOUT 3 CUPS

An indispensable Mexican condiment—some salsas are hotter than others. This one is mild and delicious. Serve some with Guacamole and tortilla chips, but reserve at least ¾ cup for Burritos.

> 3 large tomatoes, peeled and chopped
> 2 mild long green chilies, chopped
> 2 small scallions, chopped
> 1 tablespoon vinegar
> 1 small clove garlic, crushed
> 1 teaspoon chopped fresh coriander (cilantro) or 1 table-spoon chopped Italian parsley
> Salt and freshly ground black pepper to taste

Mix all ingredients thoroughly and, if possible, allow to stand an hour or so at room temperature for flavors to blend.

Burritos

MAKES 16 BURRITOS

Guests will enjoy assembling their own burritos by selecting whatever combination of flavors and textures appeals to them.

> 16 Flour Tortillas (recipe below)
> Chicken Filling (recipe below)
> Refried Bean Filling (recipe below)
> About 1½ cups Guacamole
> 1 small head iceberg lettuce, shredded
> About 2 cups Monterey Jack or mild Cheddar cheese, coarsely grated
> About ¾ cup Salsa Cruda

The tortillas should be served warm, wrapped in a clean napkin or towel to retain the heat. First put a generous amount of chicken or bean filling in center of tortilla. The choice of garnishes is largely a matter of personal preference, but the chicken filling is more highly seasoned than the bean, and therefore requires less additional flavor. For chicken burritos you might wish to add just a generous tablespoon of Guacamole and some shredded lettuce. For bean burritos add a tablespoon of cheese, a teaspoon of Salsa Cruda and/or a tablespoon of Guacamole, and some shredded lettuce. Fold top and bottom of burrito over filling and fold over sides.

Note: Other garnishes for burritos include sour cream, finely chopped tomato, thinly sliced scallions, finely minced onion, finely chopped ripe olives, and sliced radishes.

Flour Tortillas
MAKES 8 TORTILLAS

A specialty of the north of Mexico, these versatile pancake-flat breads are also popular in Texas and California for delicious quick lunches and snacks. Flour tortillas are not as widely available in stores as the more familiar corn tortillas, but fortunately they are not difficult to prepare at home. Make two batches for the Burrito Party, so that each guest can have one chicken burrito and one bean burrito. These freeze well, so it is a good idea to make them in advance and have a ready supply in your freezer.

2 cups all-purpose flour
¾ teaspoon salt
½ cup butter or margarine
About ½ cup water

In a bowl combine flour and salt and then cut in butter or margarine, using a pastry blender or two knives, until mixture resembles fine crumbs. Add water and stir until moistened. If necessary add 1 or 2 tablespoons more water. Knead dough gently for a few minutes. It should be moist but firm. Divide into eight portions and shape in balls. Cover with a damp paper towel and let stand 15 to 20 minutes. (Cover dough completely to avoid drying out.)

On lightly floured surface roll out each ball into 9- to 10-inch circle. Stack circles and cover with damp towel. Heat large skillet or griddle until very hot. Do not add oil. Bake tortillas one at a time until blistered and blisters brown. Turn quickly with a spatula, and cook on other side. Make an envelope of folded foil and slip tortillas into it as they are cooked to keep warm. (Or cool wrapped in foil envelope. To freeze, wrap airtight in freezer foil. Reheat wrapped tortillas in 250° F. oven to serve.)

Chicken Filling
FILLS 8 TORTILLAS
2½- to 3-pound chicken, quartered
2½ teaspoons salt
1 small onion
2 tablespoons vegetable oil
1 medium onion, finely chopped
1 clove garlic, crushed or pressed
8-ounce can whole tomatoes, chopped
1 tablespoon white vinegar
¼ teaspoon black pepper
¼ teaspoon oregano

Put chicken in saucepan and cover with cold water. Add 2 teaspoons salt and small onion and bring water to a boil. Reduce heat, cover, and simmer for 1 hour. Lift chicken pieces out of broth and cool. (Skim broth and freeze for later use.) Skin and bone chicken and shred meat. In a frying pan, heat oil over medium-high heat. Add chopped onion and garlic and cook quickly. Add tomatoes, vinegar, ½ teaspoon salt, pepper, and oregano and simmer for about 5 minutes. Add shredded chicken and cook for 5 more minutes. Serve warm.

Refried Bean Filling
FILLS 8 TORTILLAS
2 cups dried pinto beans (see note)
8 cups water
2 teaspoons salt
3 tablespoons vegetable oil
1 small onion, chopped fine
1 clove garlic

Rinse beans and put in large saucepan. Add water and salt and bring to a boil. Reduce heat, cover, and simmer for 2 to 2¼ hours until beans are tender. Drain and reserve liquid.

In a heavy skillet, heat oil over medium-high heat, reduce heat, add beans ½ cup at a time, and mash thoroughly with spoon. Add onion and garlic and stir. Reduce heat to low and cook beans until they are a thick paste, adding a small amount of bean cooking liquid if too dry. Serve warm.

Note: Canned pinto beans may be substituted for the cooked dried beans.

Caramel Flan
SERVES 8

In Mexico and Puerto Rico flan is often made with evaporated milk, and it produces a rich, delectable custard. Make this the day before you serve it.

Caramel
½ cup sugar
2 tablespoons water

Custard
6 eggs
2 egg yolks
½ cup sugar
⅛ teaspoon salt
Two 13-ounce cans evaporated milk
2 teaspoons vanilla extract

First caramelize the mold. In a small heavy-bottomed pan combine ½ cup sugar with 2 tablespoons water and boil over moderate heat until sugar melts and syrup turns a rich golden brown. Do not let syrup get too dark. Pour caramel into a 2-quart mold or soufflé dish and tilt mold to distribute the caramel evenly around the sides and bottom of the dish.

Preheat oven to 325° F. Beat eggs and yolks until well blended and pale lemon-colored. Add ⅔ cup sugar and the salt and beat to mix thoroughly. Beat in milk and vanilla. Strain into caramelized mold. Place mold in a shallow baking pan that has been filled with hot water. (Put pan on oven rack and then fill with water.) Bake in oven 45 minutes to 1 hour, or until knife inserted in center of flan comes out clean. Cool and then refrigerate. Place a serving dish over the mold and invert to serve.

Sangría
MAKES 1½ QUARTS, SERVES 4

1 tablespoon sugar
1 quart dry red wine
1 orange, thinly sliced and seeded
1 lemon, thinly sliced and seeded
1 peach, peeled and thinly sliced
12-ounce bottle club soda

Put sugar in large glass pitcher. Add wine and stir to dissolve sugar. Add orange and lemon slices and let stand for at least an hour. To serve add peach slices, ice cubes, and club soda. (You will need 2 pitchers or 3 quarts of sangría to serve eight.)

Licuado de Piña (Pineapple Drink)
SERVES 8 TO 10

2 small ripe pineapples
2 quarts water
1 cup sugar

Peel pineapples and remove eyes. Cut into small bits and blend in batches in blender. Combine pineapple, water, and sugar and steep for 3 to 4 hours. Chill in refrigerator. Serve in tall glasses over ice.

▸Middle Eastern Pita Sandwich Party

This is probably the easiest party ever. Although the food is different and delicious, everything but the lamb kofta can be prepared in advance. This robust and hearty fare seems especially suitable for entertaining in late summer or early autumn. Here is one meal that should have both hosts and guests dancing in the aisles.

> *Herbed Feta Cheese
> Greek Olives
> *Lentil Salad
> *Middle Eastern Lamb Kofta in Pita Bread
> Black Grapes, Green Grapes, Walnuts, and Dates
> Roditis or Other Dry Rosé Wine
> Dark Roast Coffee

Herbed Feta Cheese
MAKES ABOUT 3 CUPS

1 pound feta cheese
1 cup olive oil or half olive oil and half safflower oil
¼ cup lemon juice
2 tablespoons minced scallions, including some of the green tops
1 medium clove garlic, minced (optional)
½ teaspoon oregano
½ teaspoon salt
¼ teaspoon black pepper

Cut feta into ¾-inch cubes and place in a glass or pottery bowl. Combine oil, lemon juice, scallions, garlic, oregano, salt, and pepper and pour over cheese. Cover bowl with plastic wrap and marinate cheese squares for at least 2 hours. To serve drain cheese and spear each cube with a toothpick.

Lentil Salad
SERVES 8

¾ pound dried lentils
½ teaspoon salt
¼ teaspoon black pepper
1 cup chopped parsley
1 cup chopped scallions
Vinegar and oil to taste
2 large tomatoes, chopped and drained
Armenian flatbread or other crackers

Wash lentils and place them in a saucepan with enough water to cover. Bring to a boil, then lower heat and simmer for 15 minutes. Drain the lentils, return them to the saucepan, and re-fill pan with cold water. Add salt and pepper. Bring to a boil, then lower heat and simmer until lentils are tender, 40 to 45 minutes. Drain lentils and chill them. To serve, combine lentils, parsley, scallions, vinegar, and oil. Toss to mix thoroughly. Garnish with chopped tomato and serve with crisp Armenian flatbread or other crackers.

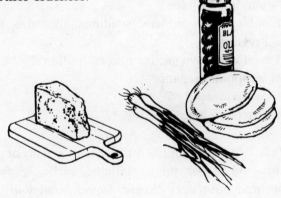

Middle Eastern Lamb Kofta in Pita Bread
MAKES 8 TO 10 SANDWICHES

3 pounds ground lean lamb
1 large onion, peeled and finely chopped
½ cup bread crumbs
1½ teaspoons salt
½ teaspoon black pepper
1 teaspoon ground coriander
1 teaspoon cumin
½ teaspoon oregano
⅓ cup milk
8 to 10 large loaves Pita
1 cup chopped parsley
1 cup finely chopped scallions
Yogurt Sauce (recipe below)

In large mixing bowl combine lamb, onion, bread crumbs, salt, pepper, coriander, cumin, oregano, and milk. Mix ingredients with your hands or with a spoon until well blended. Moisten hands with warm water and form the mixture into 24 sausage shapes 2 inches long and ¾ inch in diameter. Arrange sausages in a large baking dish and bake for 1 hour in a 375° F. oven. Turn kofta as they cook to make sure they brown evenly. To serve, place 2 or 3 kofta in pita pocket and top with parsley and scallions or with Yogurt Sauce.

Yogurt Sauce
1 cup plain yogurt, at room temperature
¼ cup finely chopped cucumber
¼ cup finely chopped scallions
Salt and white pepper to taste

Combine the above ingredients and mix thoroughly.

▸ Soup and Sandwich Supper

The Dutch are famous for their robust appetites and their hearty split pea soup. And the ideal partner for this Dutch treat is Old-Fashioned Ham Salad Sandwiches. Make the soup the day before your supper.

    Celery, Carrot, and Green Pepper Sticks
*Dutch Split Pea Soup
*Old-Fashioned Ham Salad Sandwiches
    Dark Beer
*Apple Crisp

Dutch Split Pea Soup
SERVES 8

3 cups dried green split peas
3 quarts water
3 small smoked ham hocks
3 small leeks
2 onions
2 tablespoons butter or vegetable oil
2 tablespoons chopped parsley
2 ribs celery, including leaves
½ bay leaf
¼ teaspoon freshly ground black pepper
Salt to taste

Rinse split peas under cold water and place in large soup kettle with water and ham hocks. Bring to a boil, reduce heat so that soup just simmers, cover, and simmer for 2 hours. Clean and slice leeks and onions. Heat butter or oil in frying pan and sauté leeks and onions until tender but not brown. Add to peas with parsley, celery, bay leaf, and pepper. Simmer, covered, for

1 hour, stirring occasionally to prevent burning. Remove from heat and let stand until lukewarm. Remove the ham hocks, shred the meat, and discard the bones. Return meat to soup, adjust the seasonings, and reheat until piping hot.

Old-Fashioned Ham Salad Sandwiches
MAKES 8 SANDWICHES

3 cups coarsely cut cooked ham
1 small onion, quartered
3 tablespoons chopped dill pickle
Mayonnaise
2 tablespoons spicy brown mustard
Freshly ground black pepper to taste
16 slices whole wheat bread or White Wheat Germ Bread
8 romaine lettuce leaves, shredded

In a blender whirl ham, half a cup at a time, until chopped fine. Transfer to bowl. Chop onion in blender and add to ham. Add chopped pickle and toss to blend. Combine ¾ cup mayonnaise and mustard in a small dish and add to ham mixture. Stir to blend thoroughly. Spread ham salad on half the bread slices and top with lettuce. Spread remaining bread slices with a small amount (about 1 teaspoon each) of mayonnaise and place on top of lettuce.

Apple Crisp

SERVES 8

3 to 4 pounds (or 8 large) cooking apples, preferably
    Granny Smith or Golden Delicious
¼ cup water
1 cup all-purpose flour
1 cup light brown sugar
¼ teaspoon salt
1 teaspoon cinnamon
½ cup (1 stick) butter or margarine

Peel, core, and slice apples and place in a buttered 2-quart casserole. Sprinkle water over apples. In a bowl combine flour,
sugar, salt, and cinnamon. With a pastry blender or two knives
cut in butter until mixture is a crumbly consistency, then
spoon evenly over apples. Cover and bake in a preheated
350° F. oven for 30 minutes. Uncover and bake for another 30
minutes.

INDEX

173

Egg(s), 4
 Anchovy and Sliced, 139
 Denver Sandwiches, 117–18
 Gefülltes Brot, 132
 glazes for breads, 4
 Ham Soufflé, on Toast, 91–92
 hard-cooking, 32–33
 Mayonnaise, Blender, 27–28
  variations, 28–29
 Salad:
  and Bologna on White, 43
  Curried, on Sourdough, 54
  Ham and, Roll, 42
  other sandwich suggestions,
   54–55
 Sardine and:
  Broiled, on Pumpernickel, 96–97
  Spread on Whole Wheat, 60
Entertaining, sandwich parties for
  year-round, x, 140–72
Escabeche de Cebolla (Pickled
  Onions), 134–35

Falafel in Pita, 128–29
Feta Cheese:
 Fried, on Pita, 126
 Herbed, 167–68
 in Pita, 65–66
Finnish-Style Health Bread, 18–19
 cold sandwiches on, 48, 54, 61, 64,
  67, 69
Fish:
 on a Bun with Green Sauce, 97
 Poached, 59
 Salad Rolls, 59
 see also specific types of fish
Flan, Caramel, 165
Flour, 3
 see also Breads; Cake, seed; Cook-
  ies; Tortillas
Frankfurter(s), 83–88
 Bacon-Cheese Dogs, 88
 cooking directions, 84
 Crusty Corn Dogs, 88
 Hot Dogs with All the Trimmings,
  148–49
 Mustard, Parmesan, 86
 with Onion Chili Sauce, 86–87
 with Peppers and Onions, 85
 -Sauerkraut Roll-Ups, 87
 with Special Sauerkraut, 85–86
 Texas Chili Dogs, 115
 see also Sausage
Frankfurter rolls:
 cold sandwiches on 40–41, 103

hot sandwiches on, 104
 frankfurters on, 85–86, 88, 115,
  148–49
French Bread:
 cold sandwiches on, 39–40, 124, 132,
  135
 hot sandwiches on, 81–82, 93–94,
  100–101, 107–9, 112, 114, 135
French Rolls:
 cold sandwiches on, 120, 124
 hot sandwiches on, 130–31
Fruit, see specific types of fruit

Garlic:
 Butter, 26
  Green, 76
 Mayonnaise, 28
 Muffuletta, 113
 Pan Bagna, 124
 Peruvian Buttifarras, 134
Garnishes, 30
Gefülltes Brot, 132
Genoa Salami, Muffuletta, 113
Ginger:
 Dressing, Soy-, 158
 Ice Cream, 158–59
Golden Cornmeal Yeast Bread, 13
 cold sandwiches on, 55, 67, 69
Gorgonzola, 64
Gouda Cheese, French-Toasted Ham
  and, 91
Grapefruit, Sliced Strawberries and,
  Sections in Orange Juice, 142
Green Chilies, see Chilies, Green
Green Garlic Butter, 76
Green Mayonnaise, 28
Green Pepper(s):
 Onion-, Topping, 74
Green Peppercorn Mayonnaise, 29
Green Sauce, 97
Gruyère Cheese:
 Croque Monsieur, 123
 Sauce, 143
Guacamole, 160
 Bacon, and Tomato on a Muffin, 68
 Burritos, 161–62
 Topping, 75

Ham:
 and Apple Roll-Ups, 40–41
 and Asparagus:
  on Muffins with Cheese Sauce,
   142
  Roll-Ups, 40
 Barbecued, in Pita, 93